D1808365

Simon, wins
Service wins
every time!
With gratitude,
Martha

IT CAN BE DONE

"*WHY?* is filled with relatable rants about a subject Martha Humler knows well: customer service. My wish is one day stories like these will be few and far between—but in the meantime, I hope Martha's book gives you a giggle."
—**Ken Blanchard, coauthor of *The One Minute Manager*®, *Legendary Service*, and *Raving Fans***

"Martha's stories are a lighthouse of actionable insights for service professionals that are swimming in a sea of mediocrity."
—**Dr. John Timmerman, Chief Scientist, Customer Experience & Innovation, Gallup**

"Delivering service excellence is a powerful differentiator across industries. Martha Humler's gallery in *WHY?* makes for both an educational and entertaining read".
—**Toni Belloni, Group Managing Director, LVMH**

"Service is at the heart of who we are as human beings. We are always trying to please somebody else by serving them, and that's the driving force of success for any business. The key to perfect service in the hospitality industry is in Martha's book."
—**José Andrés, Chef/Owner of ThinkFoodGroup**

"In *WHY?*, Martha Humler brings an expert's eye to the most fundamental of questions in the service industry. Her insights will have readers (and employees, employers, and everyone else in the service chain) wondering, *'Why didn't I think of that?'*"
—**Bruce Wallin, Editorial Director, Robb Report**

"Martha Humler has written a deceptively important book. Deceptive, because she's used her searing wit and iconic humor to create a book that would be worth reading simply for the pure pleasure of her language, but which goes much further to offer real insights and practical advice on the topic of service that anyone, in any industry, will find valuable."
—**Jim Huling, Managing Consultant, FranklinCovey**

"In today's chaotic world, the Customer is Boss – and most businesses couldn't care less, which is why they will be disrupted and displaced. "Never give the customer what they want. Give them what they never dreamed possible." — Growth and Prosperity await businesses that practice this. Martha's *WHY?* brings this to life — and will make you laugh out loud too."
—**Kevin Roberts, Chairman, Saatchi & Saatchi Worldwide; Head Coach, Publicis**

WHY?

BECAUSE YOU GET PAID TO SMILE AND SERVE

Written by Martha Humler

Book Illustrations by Simon Goodway
Brand Logo by Carolyn Belefski

ARCHWAY
PUBLISHING

Copyright © 2016 Martha Humler.
Author photo © Lori Lefkowitz Photography

All rights reserved. No part of this book may be used or reproduced by
any means, graphic, electronic, or mechanical, including photocopying,
recording, taping or by any information storage retrieval system
without the written permission of the author except in the case of
brief quotations embodied in critical articles and reviews.

Archway Publishing books may be ordered through booksellers or by contacting:

Archway Publishing
1663 Liberty Drive
Bloomington, IN 47403
www.archwaypublishing.com
1 (888) 242-5904

Because of the dynamic nature of the Internet, any web addresses or
links contained in this book may have changed since publication and
may no longer be valid. The views expressed in this work are solely those
of the author and do not necessarily reflect the views of the publisher,
and the publisher hereby disclaims any responsibility for them.

Any people depicted in stock imagery provided by Thinkstock are models,
and such images are being used for illustrative purposes only.
Certain stock imagery © Thinkstock.

Interior Graphics: Simon Goodway

This book is a work of non-fiction. Unless otherwise noted, the author
and the publisher make no explicit guarantees as to the accuracy of
the information contained in this book and in some cases, names of
people and places have been altered to protect their privacy.

ISBN: 978-1-4808-3834-5 (sc)
ISBN: 978-1-4808-3835-2 (hc)
ISBN: 978-1-4808-3836-9 (e)

Library of Congress Control Number: 2016916863

Print information available on the last page.

Archway Publishing rev. date: 11/3/2016

DEDICATION

How does one decide to whom a book should be dedicated? You are certain to hurt someone's feelings, are you not? Maybe if you plan to write a series, you can be assured that you will get to all the important folks in your life by the fourteenth volume. The problem is that I don't intend to write a series.

To make certain that no one significant in my life could feel slighted, I decided the solution was to dedicate the book to beloved deceased people.

I dedicate this writing adventure to my dad and four wonderful grandparents. Three of my grandparents showed through example the epitome of commitment you must have to be successful in any service industry. The fourth, my Grammy Gonya, taught me that work at home is an equally demanding service-driven operation and we should always have a garden in our lives. And my dad, who had to step into their shoes and taught me how important it is to give up the bottom line when it means helping a friend in need.

May they be looking down and chuckling.

CONTENTS

"Does it make you backward if you
read the foreword at the end?"

FOREWORD

I have been asked to write many forewords and endorsements over the years. While I am always happy to promote a good read, my reason for offering to write a foreword for Martha's book is different. I don't want to go hungry.

Why? is a laugh-out-loud slant on the mishaps we all encounter throughout many of our day-to-day interactions with all types of businesses providing services. She is spot-on when describing the mediocrity we endure. If you can stand back, after you level out your blood pressure, you will agree that we all have an uphill road to climb to receive acceptable customer service assistance in so many industries.

Why? draws attention to the work we have to do. But as Martha's tag prompts us, both in business (and home, where she reminds me often) it can be done. Let's start with speaking up when things aren't going well, taking advantage of the numerous websites available to voice our praise or disappointment, and only frequenting the establishments that do it well—politely and efficiently serving us.

Enjoy *Why?* We can all relate to many of the stories in the book. More importantly, join Martha in continuing her service revolution to demand better service, whether grabbing a cup of coffee, purchasing a home appliance, picking up dry cleaning, or applying for Medicare. It can and should be done.

Herve Humler, president and chief operations officer,
The Ritz-Carlton Hotel Company

PREFACE

Honestly I don't often read the front matter with Roman numerals in books. I usually start on page one. But since many readers do start right at the beginning, let me share how this book came into being.

I never intended to be an author. Writing is such an isolated endeavor. I'm a people person. I am the girl who

- could never quite achieve an exemplary in conduct because she was always talking in class,
- has the human development degree and twenty-five years in human resources,
- was once told at her annual performance review session that she had potential but people were not going to take her seriously, resulting in the potential of being held back, and
- became the young woman who continued her way to achieving a vice president title at a twenty-six-store retail chain at a time when women were not often recognized.

For the latter, thank you, Bill and Barbara.

But that is how this venture began. Since I've been told I tell a funny story, I took a crack at committing some of them to page. Suddenly there were service mishaps everywhere that were making their way into the book. Because most businesses are providing some type of service, the opportunities to address blunders from a variety of industries were endless. Universally speaking the same principles apply.

You won't find it hard to believe that there are already a dozen stories for the second edition of *Why?* Each of you can probably write your own book of rants. Perhaps some of mine will inspire a reader or two to join the service revolution and demand better. It can be done.

ACKNOWLEDGMENTS

My thanks and gratitude to everyone who listened, laughed, gave me story ideas, or never read a page but gave supportive coaching. To Herve, thanks for enthusiastically playing along, my love. Ava, when you laughed, I knew it was good to go in. Luke, the best compliment was hearing you tell others it was pretty good. Simon Goodway, it was jolly good fun working with you. Carolyn Belefski, fifty shades of red later, we got it. Hannah Davis, my biggest fan and best story enhancer. Betty Surrency and Mary Campbell, my guiding family counselors. Mom and Larry (may God rest his soul), ever the encouraging parents. Carol and Roy, indulging me with listening and laughing. Roxanna Pierce, my best advisor, even if I didn't always follow it. Colleen Evans, you continue to give me invaluable ideas to launch. Amy Mehlman, you reminded me to tell the other side. Kate and Norm Tardif, you laid the framework for the bathroom story. Pat and Mike Guinzali, you started me on the banking segment. Nell McCarty, dotting the i's on the very first pass. Martine Bernard, I needed a good word tweaker. Martha Deane, you listened, laughed and taught me to foreword march, or is it forward? Steve McLean, marketing extraordinaire, for the idea to make Why? wedge-shaped to double as a door stop. Erin Donovan, you know why. And, Peter Greenberg, with whom I lost my radio virginity.

INTRODUCTION

I love the question of why. When asked, it denotes an answer of explanation is requested. That is the reason the title of each chapter includes the why question and then my sometimes sarcastic response. I leave it up to you, the reader, to ponder the rest of the why question.

So why me? What qualifies me to write a book about service? Well, there are several reasons actually. First, I am at the age where I can say whatever I want. It is so freeing. Also like all of you, I am a consumer, and when I am spending money and utilizing the various services offered to me, I deserve to get friendly and efficient assistance. I witnessed firsthand in my varied career in human resources that service will trump. Companies that believe in service, fund internal training, and provide all levels of staff with proper instruction will be the winners.

I am also married to one of the kings of hospitality. Come to think of it, maybe that is why I like him. I finally found someone who believes, as I do, that the employees who interface with the customer are indeed the face of any company. And that training and communication are essential to ensure employees understand their role in the service mission.

Every story I cite is the absolute truth of a situation that indeed happened, but no names are divulged. You can try to guess, but my lips are sealed.

The vignettes are random, not laid out in any order of importance. In fact, they are in order of when each situation came across my radar and I wrote them down.

Readers will see here the ridiculousness in the far-reaching lack of service standards, but I also know what it takes to get it right. While I was determined to not write yet another leadership resource book, many subtle hints and sometimes blunt directives are found throughout.

So hold on to your hats. I think I have taken an objective look at an assortment of establishments that should be concerned with service, pleasantly and efficiently assisting you and me.

It's sort of funny (not really) that the majority of the stories I mention occurred within the last year. I had been thinking of writing a tell-all for a very long time. Lord knows there is always material out there. But I just recently started consciously studying and taking notes. Had I been jotting down observations and mishaps for several years, you would be enjoying a five-volume series!

"You want one larger than this?"

CHAPTER 1
WHY? BECAUSE IT IS IN MY BLOOD

I learned the importance of customer service at a young age. Both of my parents were shop owners. I was pushed into our friends' jewelry store at fourteen and paid each week under the diamond counter to wrap gifts at Christmas time. I made my way up the ladder to engraving when I could be paid legally and continued on while in high school. I got the end-all-be-all job in the jewelry store chain of promotions. I was permitted to sell diamonds at age seventeen! What a day that was. I was puffed up like a peacock with my advancement.

It all fell apart a few weeks later. The couple I was showing diamonds to stole one while I had my back turned to get another tray of styles. That is another book in itself. Identifying a suspect in a police lineup at age seventeen gave me nightmares for years.

I digress. I'll go back to my parents. Our dinner conversations invariably turned to business. Business is up; business is down. They lived and breathed business. I am not really even sure they noticed when I left for college.

I learned that customers could be demanding and obnoxious but the shopkeeper still needed to smile and satisfy their needs. In turn, my mother taught me to expect good service from others.

She would think nothing of insisting that the vacation lobster pound remove excess water from the scale before placing our picks inside. She certainly was not going to pay extra for someone else's water weight!

By far, this is the best story. Again while on vacation, Mom went to the closest corner store for two essential items.

"Excuse me. Do you carry Milkbone dog biscuits?" my mother asked.

"Over there," the shopkeeper curtly replied while half-heartedly pointing toward the aisles.

"Thank you. And do you carry B&M baked beans?" asked Mom.

"Over there, lady," the woman stated abruptly while using her head as a pointer in the general direction.

Well, "over there" is not very helpful in a four-aisle store that you are not familiar with, so Mom decided to give her some advice, "You know, my husband and I are both in the service business. So were our parents. If we spoke to our customers like you are speaking to me, they wouldn't come back!"

And the shopkeeper retorted, "I've got a shotgun in the back, lady, and I'm not afraid to shoot it."

What more could Mom sheepishly say but, "How much do I owe you, miss?"

Evidently not all advice is welcome, but picturing my mother's face and envisioning her zigzagging all the way to her car for fear of being taken out has kept us laughing for forty years!

The stage was set for me. I was destined for a career path that was service oriented and customer driven. Perhaps it is my imagination, but it seems customer service is given less emphasis in most organizations these days. Perhaps after reading you will join my quest. It is time for a service revolution!

"Certainly seems like it will be better than yours!"

CHAPTER 2

WHY? BECAUSE YOU SHOULD TRY TO BE NICE

I don't know how anyone who doesn't smile and look happy could be hired for a job that requires being face-to-face with other people. Do you?

Haven't you experienced this? I shake my head at the apparent lack of caring every time I order a coffee, pay for groceries, enter a mail center, need to ask a question of a pharmacist, or shop for flowers at the nursery, for that matter. These people signed up for this, a job that innately requires assisting customers.

How can you not be happy knowing you are providing the eye-opening cup of joe to some sleepy-eyed customers? Who can't be smiling all day working with flowers?

If they cringe so much at contact with people, why didn't they sign up for a job in a cubicle or strive to become the next van Gogh? Now there is a solo job most of the time. Better yet, why didn't the management of these companies do a better job during the interview process?

I don't know. Is there a test for friendliness that could be added in to the interview? Wait. There is—those personality tests many companies are promoting these days. I am having a hard time buying into this being an effective tool for matching job seekers to specific positions.

But if I did decide to jump on the bandwagon, is there

a way that these advanced sophisticated computers could design a smile ability tool for applicants? Here's a decent measurement scale:

1. Lips pursed and ready to attack
2. Lips flatline
3. Intermittent smirking
4. Lips in a smile shape with no teeth
5. Broad smile with teeth visible

Bingo! Only hire the fives, please!

How about the movies? That bothers me. Where do they get those employees working the concession stands? How much fun is it to enhance someone's movie-going experience with a little popcorn and a drink? Why can't they smile more?

They must get perks, like taking turns to sneak into the back of the theaters for a few minutes or having a little cup of popcorn behind the counter to munch on. Come on, people. Have fun!

This is just one example of several entry-level jobs that are at or just above minimum wage. Stop right there. If you feel it is difficult to be motivated when holding a job with a similar pay scale, we are not on the same page. I said no names, but I can easily provide a list of companies who truly depend on these folks. What makes the difference? When their leadership lets them know how important they are to the organization, the employees feel valued.

In addition to encountering frowns or blank faces, lack of eye contact when entering an establishment is another turn-off. I notice it in a lot of retail stores, but it really bothers me in restaurants. That hostess or maître d' is on the front line.

Smile. Look up from your seating chart, and make eye contact!

"How many in your party?" really irks me. If he or she would just look up, the question would be, "Table for four?"

Besides being friendly and having the ability to smile, people dealing with the public have to be able to talk. Recently at a yogurt shop, I had to ask the young man behind the counter to repeat everything two or three times.

His lips and mouth never moved a muscle.

It was like he was practicing to be a ventriloquist.

Evidently he must have forgotten that the trick to success is to not move your lips and still have audible sounds coming out!

"How in the world did he get hired for this job?" I asked myself as I left.

I concluded that he must have been the owner's son, the only possible theory to justify why he was employed there.

Oh, this lack of associate friendliness doesn't always hold firm. I know that.

There are pockets of helpful, friendly, efficient establishments, but that would be a short book.

"Yoo-hoo! Anyone home?"

CHAPTER 3

WHY? BECAUSE SOMEONE HAS TO OPEN THE DOORS ... OR DO THEY?

We consumers face another scenario when we are out spending our hard-earned money.

Is anyone working there? Can you find a breathing body to help you after you have helped yourself to find what you needed and just want to pay?

Did I miss the sign saying the second floor is closed on Tuesdays?

Did they hold a class on ringing up your own sale that I should have attended?

It has become a game of hide-and-seek.
"Come out. Come out,
wherever you are!"

Yes, it's true. Companies are cutting bodies to the point of no return.

But here is the counter question: what are people going to do for gainful employment? I am posing another why question here, folks.

Have you noticed how many establishments are evolving to self-checkout? I now have self-checkout at the drugstore, grocery store, gas station, bank, airline, and building parking lots, to name a few.

At least I see my smiling face in the screen reflection while checking myself out. And I get a five on my smile test!

**"I slipped a lollipop through the
slit. Have a great day!"**

CHAPTER 4

WHY? BECAUSE WE ARE PAYING TO BE SERVED

So now I ask you: how would you rank the service level you receive these days?

I leave the retail establishments out of this category. I am talking about companies that don't sell goods, but whose function provides us with a service.

Think restaurants, hospitals, insurance companies, utility companies, package and postal carriers, and moving businesses. You get the idea. How about throwing in state and federal agencies and our local governments while we are at it?

Allow me to launch in.

Let's start with restaurants. For the most part, restaurants understand that service and good food are paramount to their success. Certainly the high-end establishments have it down better than the less pricey chains and fast-food outlets. But I don't care where a restaurant falls on the affordability scale. People have chosen to use their disposable income on a night out, and they deserve an evening of fun and good food without having to point out dirty silverware.

This has to have happened to you at some point. Man, unclean utensils make me want to eat with my hands—at least I know the last time I washed them.

Someone forgot to educate the dishwashers that, even though they might not think their job is significant, it is one of the key roles in the heart of the house. The folks washing the dishes need to know how vital they are to a smooth food operation.

I am not sure if you picked up on it, but I mentioned the dishwasher works in the heart of the house, a phrase coined by my husband's company. I smiled when I picked up on this significant word change at his company that clearly indicates these jobs are not at the back of the house, as they were referred to for years. What a wonderful acknowledgment of how important each and every job in an organization is.

If you work in the heart of the house, you are critical to the successful functioning of the business.

This doesn't just apply to restaurants. There are so many examples of how an organization's behind-the-scenes workforce impacts how the customer forms an opinion of a company.

Here's a good example.

What company sends out their repair team for a job without a myriad of tools that they may need for the repair? That has happened to me several times. Did they want to drive the thirty minutes to my home just to assess and come back seventeen days later? What a misuse of efficiency.

I waited (forever) for a company to come to repair two cabinet hinges on a new closet system. The service technician arrived at the door with nothing—literally nothing—to work with.

"Oh, hello. I am here for your closet repair. May I take a look?"

Of course I assumed after the look-see that he would be going out to his massive van to retrieve all he needed to do the repair.

"Okay. I see what I need to do. Why don't you call the office for a second appointment, and I will bring out what I need?"

What is in the massive van? I pondered. *Does he double as a florist, and is it filled with arrangements he is delivering in between his closet repair stops?*

No way, fella.

Thank goodness I had a ladder and a screwdriver, so he got half of the job accomplished. There would still be a second trip, but at least a cabinet door wouldn't impair us in the meantime.

I loved the closet sales rep. The installation crew were very good as well. But herein lies a breakdown in so many companies. They forget to train everyone that:

"After the sale, it's the service that counts."

This was the slogan at my parents' appliance store forty years ago. It is as meaningful today as it was then, don't you agree?

"Kids, you are having napkins and
mustard for lunch today."

Oh, the drive thru joints. I actually love them when they run efficiently.

Unfortunately I have learned never to leave the window without opening the bag and making sure we have everything we ordered. Surely this has happened to you. Even if you were lucky enough that the food order is all correct, something is always missing.

Here I think:

- Oops! No straws. *Well, don't they come automatically when you order drinks with lids?*
- Oops! No sauce. *It said honey mustard on your screen.*
- Oops! Boy toy. *You asked me, "Boy or girl?"*

As I said, I refuse to drive away until a thorough inventory check is conducted. My kids are totally embarrassed that I am "holding up the line" but I got tired of driving away, only to have to peel into a parking spot to run inside with my list of missing items.

Someone is not monitoring to ensure they have an efficient assembly line plan for the takeout window.

"Who did he bribe for that bread basket?"

Not only are establishments cutting back on bodies, but what is up with the cuts in bread and shopping bags? Seriously now, was there a covert meeting I missed where the leaders of the free world announced an edict?

NO bodies ... NO bread ... NO bags.

Really? How much does it cost to serve up a few rolls in a restaurant? Maybe if you are trying to shed a few pounds, you like the fact that you won't be tempted. Your hand won't be able to reach into the lined basket and feel the warm, soft objects. You won't have to worry about carefully cradling this delectable morsel to your dish, and you don't have to be bothered with choosing among the various seasoned olive oils that have been presented at your table.

But I want one!

Some businesses have heightened the anticipation of the arrival of the breadbasket with creative flat breads, infused cheeses, spiced sticks, and to-die-for spreads and oils. My mouth is watering just writing about it. Unless someone requests "No bread, please," I say, "Bring it on." Please don't charge us for it. That really miffs me.

"No need to hit the gym today."

The third B is for bags.

Well, I can see no bag if you grabbed a pack of gum while paying for gas. Of course you can toss it into a purse or pocket. And I also support the movement to bring in your own reusable bags in certain situations.

With that said, do you carry a bag of bags with you as you are walking down the street in town? Are you really able to think ahead to the possibility that there will be so many cute shops that you won't be able to resist purchasing a few items that will be difficult to carry back to the car? Of course not. Therefore, when you go into an establishment and get to the checkout with several items, don't you think it is odd when the cashier asks you if you want a bag?

"Oh no. I'll be fine. I'll balance the board game under one arm. Well, first I will cut open the cellophane and squeeze in the two greeting cards I bought into the game box. Do you have any tape to seal it back up? I would hate to lose some of the game pieces on my way home.

I'll tuck the new books in the sleeve of my sweater. That should hold them in place. And you are my witness that I did indeed pay for these small items that I am going to put in my pants pockets."

Of course I need a bag!

Employees don't think of these cost-saving schemes themselves. These are directives from management to save a few pennies.

A business absolutely devoted to service will have only one worry about profits.
They will be embarrassingly large.
-Henry Ford, founder, Ford Motors

"Is that my pizza?"

CHAPTER 5

WHY? BECAUSE WE NEED TO SPEAK OUT

We have a fabulous movie theater that we love to go to because they serve homemade pizzas to enjoy while you watch the show. I witnessed the cardinal sin of food handling while there, and I didn't say a thing.

An elderly gentleman, obviously on his maiden trip to the place, was very confused as to the process involved:

1. Order and pay. Take your beeper, and select a seat inside the theater.
2. When the beeper lights up, go back and find your order on a table. Use a potholder to carry it. After all, it did just come out of the oven.
3. Back inside the theater, grab your utensils. Sit. Eat. Enjoy the movie.

No one explained all this to the gentleman so he left the order line and went directly to the table. Obviously puzzled, he looked down at two whole piping hot pizzas that the chef had just placed down.

I heard him mumble something about plates, and then he reached into one of the pies and started to tear off a slice.

The manager just happened to be walking by. He took the slice from the man and placed it back on the tray,

shoving it back into the triangular opening to form the perfect whole pizza once more. He explained to the gentleman
to take the pizza on its tray back to his seat. The man was
told that plates were inside.

Again the elderly man slipped his fingers gently under the slice of pizza and pulled it out, ruining the perfect circle. Once more, the manager grabbed the slice
from the man, put it back in place, and repeated his
instructions.

Finally the gentleman explained, "But I only ordered
one slice."

"Oh," says the manager, "then go sit down and wait for
your beeper to light up."

Now I looked at the pizza pie in question, and it really
didn't show severe signs of destruction from this tug-of-
war act I had just witnessed. But I have to say something,
don't I?

So as the manager now saw that I saw and made eye
contact with me, I said, "I really feel bad for whoever ordered that pizza," thinking that was enough of a hint that
surely he would call for a new pizza to be made.

But no. He answered, "It will be all right." Really?

I was still waiting to order when, a minute later, two
young ladies approached the table to retrieve their two
pizzas. I kept an eye on the brunette making a beeline for
the one. I cringed. I waited for her reaction that indicated
she could tell her pizza was just manhandled a minute before. But her face turned into a big smile at how yummy it
was going to be.

A little voice inside of me was saying, "Tell her. Tell her."

But then I remembered my mother and the dog bones

and beans. My kids would kill me if we were banned from coming back.

Why don't we speak up? Have we resigned ourselves that this is as good as it gets?

We all have to start speaking out.

"Yes, dear, I insist. We are hosting a
utility company boycott tonight."

CHAPTER 6

WHY? BECAUSE THE PILGRIMS MADE OUT FINE

What is going on with utility company services is really perturbing me. Have you tried working with them recently? Of course you have. We all have frequent issues with them that need to be resolved, including system failures, appointment no-shows, items they said they repaired that are still not functioning, and so on.

Isn't it maddening how they are scooping up all the small local companies we grew up with and are now forcing us just to accept their terms? In the past six months, the electric company I grew up with and wrote a check to each month at the family summer house now has a new name I can't even pronounce, victim of another merger. Let me know what changes you will be implementing, fellas, and what services I can expect will no longer be available.

At this house in a small village, we always had to contract with different companies for each utility. That meant three calls for setup and service. It was three monthly bills to pay. Everything was in triplicate. It was so nice when one of the larger players forged into this area and we set up a plan with all services provided through one carrier, which also gave us Internet for the first time.

Sadly we only had one year with their very efficient, friendly service when we got a letter informing us that a huge conglomerate acquired them. Alas, it is the company that provides our service at our year-round home, and they are not so professional to deal with. *No, I thought, don't go with them. Please don't go with them.*

I am already primed for delays and subpar service when they take over in December.

I have an example of dealing with these mighty giants. I can guarantee at least twenty minutes on the phone going through the prompts to best direct the call relating to my issue. Finally I hear a human voice to talk to. I launch into my story.

Oops! I'm informed I'll be connected to the proper department.

Oops! I'm disconnected during the transfer.

Do I have the stamina to start this process again?

Screw it! I'll light candles. It's romantic. I'll write letters. Who needs a telephone? Kids, no TV. Read a book.

When considering these mergers, there has to be more analysis on how this can further diminish their service standards and efficiency if not carefully planned out. Surely they conduct periodic research with their millions of customers to seek solutions to better meet our expectations and needs. They can't possibly be reading the results.

Wait. Do they care? Might this be part of the problem? They know we need lights, phones, TVs, and Internet. So in a way, we are held hostage since they know we would have a difficult time without these services.

What do you think of boycotting the utility companies

for one year? Could we all survive and show them we want to be heard?

Is there anyone out there to start this movement? I am too tired from calling, holding, and setting up services to see this through.

"It's only 4:00 p.m. in Iowa, you know."

CHAPTER 7

WHY? BECAUSE YOU WON'T MELT AT 5:01 P.M.

Most of us live in areas where businesses are insanely open almost twelve to sixteen hours a day. While that seems excessive, at least the logic is to accommodate customers to get their to-do list accomplished when they are not working themselves.

I have a story twisted in the opposite direction. There is a nursery not too far from where I live with a very comprehensive selection of plants and flowers. I have never found such a diverse assortment anywhere else.

I love needing some fill-ins, taking the drive over, getting my cart, and perusing the outdoor aisles and greenhouses.

I learned quickly that the plants are the only thing they have going for them. Other parts of the experience—the service and inevitable sale—are not so good. That is why they are in the book.

After a hard winter, I had lost a lot in my gardens, and I was excited to replant. I made a list of what I needed to buy with some tried-and-true favorites and some new specimens to experiment with as well.

I drove over to place my large order. It was so large in fact that I went to the office first to inquire if they deliver to save me the three trips it would take to get it all home.

"Yes, we deliver," said the tall man behind the counter.

He made such a big deal about the delivery fee, repeating and stressing the specific amount. Did he think I thought they would do that for free? Come to think of it, they probably used to deliver for gratis in the 1970s. But in this day and age? Of course not.

"When do you want them delivered?" he asked.

"Friday would be great. Thank you," I said, so proud of myself for being so organized and giving them advanced notice on Monday.

"Come back late Wednesday to place your order," he said, "so no one will take the sold tags off your order and try to buy it before we deliver on Friday."

What? I thought. *Don't they have a secure hold section? Do they need police surveillance to guard my precious peonies?*

So as directed, I showed up late on Wednesday, four forty to be exact.

I parked and found myself skipping down for the heady experience of walking the aisles and selecting my plants.

Then I heard one of the employees, wearing a crisp yellow Oxford shirt, give a stern warning to a couple ahead of me, "We close at five."

I made no eye contact with her and scooted right past her. After all, I was instructed to come late Wednesday to ensure my order stayed intact.

I walked up to the next yellow Oxford-shirted employee and explained why I was there.

She looked at her watch and then at me. "We close at five."

Another yellow Oxford-shirted employee walked up from the greenhouses below to assist. I guess she joined just in case they needed to muscle me to my car.

Meanwhile, the lady at the top, playing Paul Revere with the time warning alerts, made her way down the hill to join the group.

These three yellow Oxford-shirted ladies encircled me. I began to feel like a little lamb surrounded by coyotes.

Again I explained to the coyote group that a tall man behind the counter had instructed me. Blah, blah, blah.

They escorted me to their leader. Yikes! It was the tall man I talked to during my first visit.

He stared at me blankly.

I reminded him of our history just two days ago on Monday.

He looked at the clock on the wall. "We close at five."

I know that, poop head, and I've wasted ten minutes with everyone declaring that, synchronizing their watches and checking with you. Else I would be finished placing my order and paying by now.

I was only thinking that, but it was as if he read my mind. He literally turned and walked away without saying anything more. So I turned to the three ladies. Although they started out defensively circling, they now seemed like they wanted to help.

I asked them, "Did he even answer me? Can we gather or not?"

They all shrugged.

I stomped out the door and followed him. Picture that the three coyotes have now metamorphosed into three trembling fawns and are trailing behind me, pretty much hiding behind my coattails to witness the exchange.

I stand strong. "Excuse me, but I don't think you actually answered the question. Do I have the time to place my order or not?"

He was just staring at me, and during that tense moment, one of the three ladies, Karen, peeked out from behind me and meekly volunteered to happily write down my order at this late hour and pull it all tomorrow, if it were okay with him.

He gave a half-nod.

I shook Karen's hand, thanked her for her bravery, and began rattling off my list.

And it all went well after that. Karen was very efficient and even called me to confirm some substitutions she needed to make. Delivery also went as planned.

The sad irony is that, when I start to relay the incident, I've discovered that many people refuse to patronize this beautiful garden shop. Evidently I am not the first to have a service tale to tell.

What a shame. Obviously the owner is a knowledgeable horticulturist, and the inventory selection can't be compared, but they missed the most important elements of having a business:

Welcoming the customer, satisfying the customer, and sometimes staying until a minute or two after five.

Loyal customers innately market your establishment, and dissatisfied customers will be your word-of-mouth nightmare.

As stated previously, this mentality doesn't instinctively come from the employees. It is imitated by the philosophy and actions of the leadership.

CHAPTER 8

WHY? BECAUSE THEY DESERVE BETTER

As mentioned, these vignettes are in no particular sequence of importance. I probably had just spent the day sorting out issues for my elderly parents when the notion hit me of how frustrating every interaction can be. So allow me to divert.

Everyone at some point has the task to assist in a small or larger way, for example, an elderly person with medical issues, housing concerns, and general well-being.

Somebody, please tell those employees at the insurance companies, state agencies, and federal programs that they are dealing with people who already have failing eyes, compromised hearing, and sometimes memory issues.

Do they make it so complicated so these folks can never actually get coverage? Is it a secret conspiracy to confuse them, knowing that many who placed calls and filled out forms might forget whom they called or why they wrote and give up? Or is it just insurmountable inefficiency?

I could not believe the red tape involved when helping my family members over the last few years. I am sure that many of our beloved relatives go without investigating extended coverages or applying for benefits due to it being so difficult to get through these complex processes.

Simplify, people. Simplify.

These are the folks who guided our prosperity, fought for our freedoms, and taught us our life lessons.

While you might be thinking that these agencies aren't actually tasked with providing customer service, I strongly disagree. And if it isn't explicitly discussed during their training and duration of employment, then it should be.

For goodness sake, make it easier on the aging generations, of which I will be one of in the not too distant future, to get the care and services they deserve.

So I guess I am asking for kindness, empathy, and efficient customer service in this case. Does it sound reasonable?

*Chose a job you love, and you
will never have to work a
day in your life.*
–Confucius

"Frostbite lawsuit looking promising."

CHAPTER 9

WHY? BECAUSE WE DESERVE BETTER

A s I continue on with programs that we pay for, did you know that some mail centers are closed for lunch?

How absurd is that? Just when people might be using their lunch break to mail a package or buy stamps, the sign on the building says

Closed
12:00–1:00 p.m.

Can't they eat a big breakfast and make do? Can't they tuck some snacks under the counter to combat any potential hunger pains?

I don't know about you, but I can wolf down a sandwich and a bag of chips in ten minutes flat if I have to. Why do they need a whole hour?

This "smack in the middle of prime time" closing has happened to me in three different towns. They're small towns, I grant you, but still. They literally lock the door of the building.

I watched a woman in the front of the line, waiting for the reopening at one, quite chilled as she balanced her holiday packages on a cold day in December. From my place in the line, I could see that the mail worker inside was clearly done noshing but with no intention of unlocking the door one minute before one.

Happy holidays to you too, missy, inside that warm building, I thought, *and I hope you ate so much lunch that your holiday dress is too tight and you have to wear your uniform to the party.*

Honestly, how can this be allowed? I don't think government-managed anything will work well until they make major changes. When will they recognize that guaranteed pay and benefits do not foster motivation for quality output? A work environment that pays for performance makes for stronger employee motivation.

CHAPTER 10

WHY? BECAUSE VACATIONS ARE SUPPOSED TO BE JOYFUL

Oh, the long planned out and much anticipated vacation. Don't you expect to have a wonderful happy time where everywhere you go and everything you do will be filled with joy?

How much joy do you feel when your vacation starts with a flight somewhere?

Need I say more?

I've concluded that the airlines have different training programs for employees working in first/business versus the coach cabin. I have traveled in both.

I totally feel the love in the front of the plane in first/business. Everyone is smiling, and it is such a serene ambiance. You barely have your coat off, and someone is there to offer you a drink and a hot towel.

In economy, I sense I am one of the cattle herd. The crew is moaning while they push the heavy carts up through the aisle, all the while barking, "Arms and feet in."

Ice chips are flying as they rush through the service. Drink flip tops are opening at such a rapid rate that it literally sprays the aisle seat passengers.

"She obviously didn't make the
softball team in high school.

What is their hurry? The pilot said the flight would last five hours and eighteen minutes.

I don't understand this disparity between cabins. We are only a curtain away from the Zen-like atmosphere.

I have one more thought: could anyone possibly be assigned to tidy up the restrooms just once during longer flights? The condition of them is a telling sign of whether or not you care about us passengers.

I roll my eyes when an airline brags about its safety record.

What do they think we expect, broken-down, ill-equipped machines?

Do hotels boast, "We have beds"?

Do moving van companies shout from the rooftops, "We have big trucks"?

You get my drift. No company can rest its laurels on the obvious. That is why the level of service they offer will be what sets them apart.

This is another airline mystery to me. How could a family of four check in their bags together but one is missing by the time you arrive at your destination?

Did that suitcase suddenly develop a fear of flying and hurl itself off the conveyor belt?

Could the airline snake a chain through all four bag handles so they stay together in flight? At least that way either we all get to jump into our bathing suits when we arrive or we suffer it out together, sweating in our travel clothes.

Finally why do pilots bother with their cute opening welcome comments, for example, our flight time and weather conditions at our destination? Sometimes they include what they think is a funny joke about some sports game that day and so forth. Evidently their mothers never taught them to speak up and annunciate. Can you hear a word of what they are saying? Pilots aren't the only ones making out with their microphones. I missed my train stop once thanks to the conductor's garbled instructions.

What does it mean to pre-board?
Do you get on before you get on?
-George Carlin, American comedian

"Kids, you and the dog get in the back.
I'll get a rope to secure you in."

After the family recovers from the trip, then comes the rental car retrieval, where you'll hear:

- "I'm sorry, but your flight was early, and the car scheduled for you won't be ready for at least another hour."
- "I'm sorry, but you are late so we gave your requested car to someone else. I can offer you a slightly similar vehicle."
- "I'm sorry, but your reservation was registered at our sister location six miles away. Do you need a ride there?"

To quote one of my favorite movies,

"Love (of the customer in this case) means never having to say you're sorry."

And I have one more thing about getting the rental, connecting back to the dishwasher in restaurants. No one is more important in the rental car operation than the people cleaning the cars for the next pickup. Someone please teach them to vacuum thoroughly, clean out the pockets and sleeves, and let the next pickup not have to wonder about what actually went on in the car before they got it. What company in their right mind thinks I might be hungry after my long flight and will enjoy snacking on the remaining Doritos in the opened bag in the door pocket? Seriously.

"Hmmm. Having dinner when you
arrive wasn't on the website."

Ahh, you arrive at your escape abode, where you instantly start to think,

Wait. This doesn't look like the slideshow on their website.

This isn't even the same building color.

How many years ago did they take those pictures of this bathroom?

Where did they get those shots of the ocean view? They must have snuck between those two cottages blocking our view to photograph from there.

Kids, can you identify what that possibly might be in the refrigerator?

I'll be back in a few hours. I have to find a Laundromat to wash the sheets and towels before we use them.

And don't sit on that couch until I can cover it with one of the clean sheets when I get back.

Oh, the joy! Let the vacation begin.

"Did you not see fragile on the box?"

CHAPTER 11

WHY? BECAUSE WE PAY TO HAVE PACKAGES DELIVERED IN A REASONABLE TIME FRAME AND TO THE CORRECT DESTINATION

I guarantee that every single person on the planet can name several—and I am talking many more than one here, people—blunders with mail and package delivery. It is a difficult assignment with the daily volume of letters and packages being sent to millions of locations. But this is the business they chose to be in, correct?

There are really three major players out there. Remember, I said no names, so put on your thinking caps.

One of the mail carrier giants is government-run. Oh, yes. Based on that, we want to say it is not reasonable to expect friendliness and efficiency in those joints.

Remember the pizza story? We all still need to speak up. Our taxes pay them.

Their lack of good customer service gives a leg up for the for-profit carriers to be king of the hill when they get it right.

If I were running one of these carrier companies, I would stay well-schooled on what the competition was doing and strive to do it better. I would get out more and visit some of the franchise operations to which they have given their name. Some are just bad advertising.

Just recently, I needed to redirect two packages. In one scenario, the retailer I purchased the item from did all the work for me and worked with the carrier, and there was no charge.

Aren't you taken aback when everything goes so smoothly? It must be because it happens so infrequently.

In the other situation, the merchant washed their hands of me since a tracking number had been established and referred me to the carrier, who did assist with the redirect but charged me for it even though the delivery date was still three days away.

I ask you: which merchant and which carrier do you think will get my future business? Of course the answer is the establishment that assisted and the carrier that did not charge extra for the change.

Here is a *cockah,* as my Down Easterner grandfather loved to say when he launched into a story that he was sure would make us all gasp. This story took place at one of the better franchise operations I frequent. It is a pleasant experience to do business with them. They offer services from both of the major for-profit carriers.

I stopped in to mail a box to a faraway land, literally to far-flung Tahiti. It seemed to be the associate's first time dealing with such a remote location, but she was making every attempt to get it done.

Ironically a man from one of the carrier companies, fully dressed in the familiar uniform we all know, was just hanging around. He was not in the usual rush.

You know what I am talking about when you are near one of their stops.

They dash in with the dolly, seize the packages, sprint

to the vehicle, hurl the boxes into the truck, peel out into oncoming traffic, and zoom away.

I have often wondered if they get a bonus for getting a certain number of stops done in a precise amount of time, which would explain why they seem so harried and tense.

So I wondered why this carrier employee was just hanging around. Was it a miracle that he might actually be waiting to take my box with the packages already on his truck?

Oops. It was an awkward moment. In walked the driver from the other major carrier, also in his very recognizable uniform. He was in the rushing zone I just described, and in some weird way, it was comforting that he was showing atypical behavior.

He stopped abruptly when he saw the competition.

I was barely breathing. *Would a fistfight break out? I thought. Am I far enough away to avoid possible flying package debris?*

"Hello, Bill," said the carrier who just crossed the threshold.

"Hey, Joe. How's it going?" asked the competition who had been hanging.

Wow! They know each other and civilly greet each other, I thought. So I couldn't help but compliment them, "That is so nice that you boys are so friendly."

They smiled and nodded.

Bill even held the door for Joe and assisted him to get all his packages through the door.

Again Bill came back and leaned on the counter.

This is unbelievable, I thought, that he is taking all this time to wait for my package!

Meanwhile, the manager was having trouble with her

computer when I asked her to quote me the prices of the various shipping methods.

She asked Bill if he could get shipping fees from his machine. You know the machine I refer to—that long, black thing that does everything for them except drive the truck. Yes, that thing.

He pulled it out of the belt case, looked down at it, and said, "No, I can't. I'm on break."

I almost fell over. That was why he was standing around. He was not waiting for my package. He was on his break. My bubble had popped just when I was starting to believe again.

So I had to ask in a somewhat sarcastic tone, "So you're standing in here for your break?"

"Yes," he said. "I have packages to scan, but the machine gets turned off during my break so I have to wait."

"How does that happen?" I quizzed him.

"They get turned off back at corporate," he explained.

I had never heard of such a thing, so I probed more, "Has that always been the case?"

"No," he clarified, "just in the last couple of years."

"Well," I said, "let me guess. One or two employees misused the privilege of a flexible break time, and the whole team got punished."

"Something like that I heard," he replied.

Here was this willing employee, and he couldn't help even when he wanted to.

Corporate leadership needs to get out and witness how their decisions affect those actually helping to grow their business while they interface with the customers.

*Customer service is not a
department, it's everyone's job.*
–Anonymous

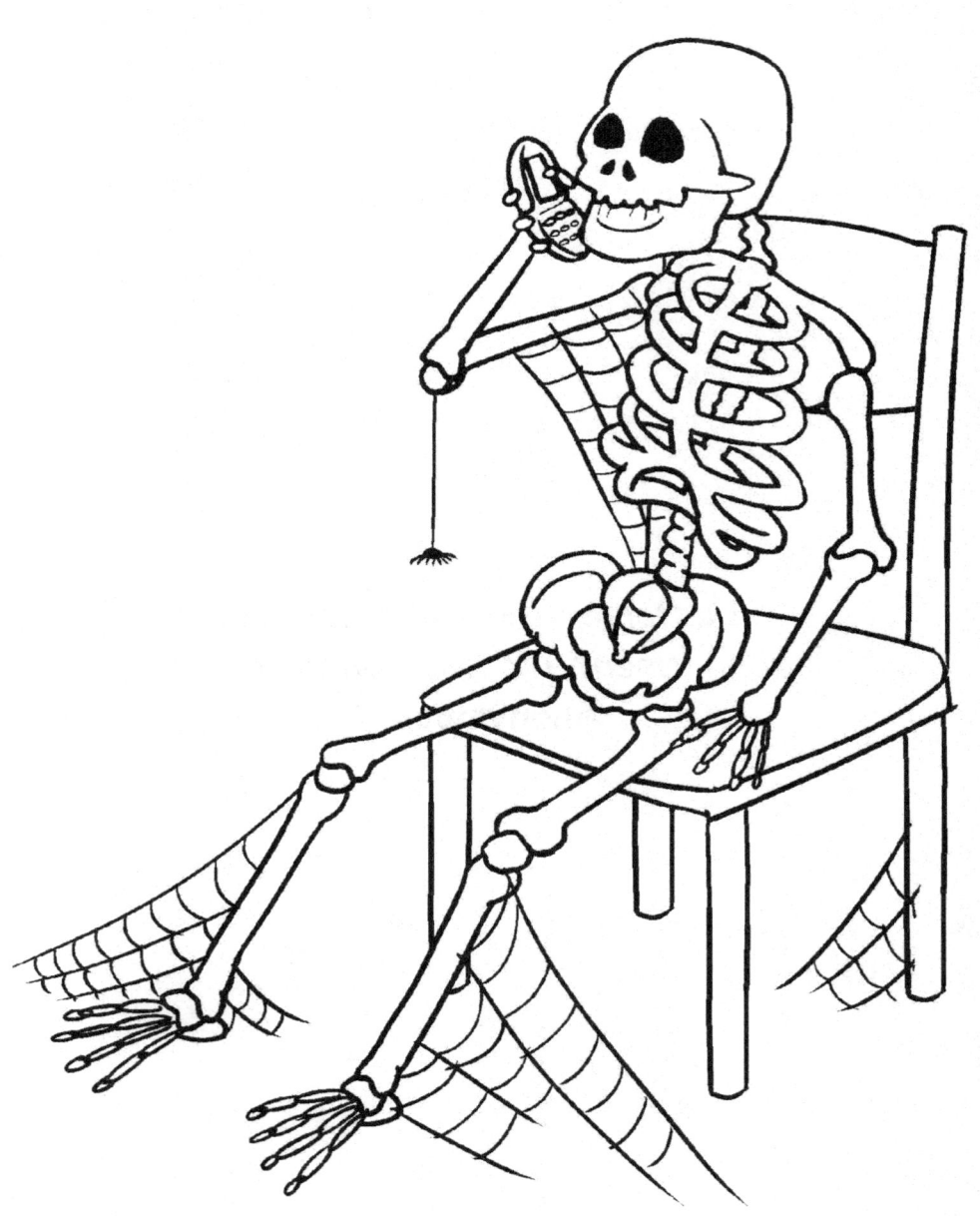

"Send my refund to charity.
I won't be needing it anymore."

CHAPTER 12

WHY? BECAUSE SURVEY SAYS DIY

Nobody seems to want to help anymore. No one is even out there to help anyway. We are on our own to figure out what to do. In other words, "do it yourself," or DIY.

I don't know about you, but I dread dealing with a situation that didn't go 100 percent as planned wherein you selected, you ordered, you paid, it arrived in a timely manner, it wasn't damaged, it looked like the photo, you are pleased, and you are keeping it. You can add your own wish list to this dream of a perfect set of circumstances.

If only this dream were a reality more often. It makes me weary just to think about embarking on the lengthy process it is sure to require when some part of the above wish list goes awry.

You try calling, usually a nightmare.

You try solving online. You reach a stage where you only have a simple question to complete the process, but you can't move forward without filling it in. You click on the "contact us" icon, which leads to a little box for you to write your question or explain your issue, which will be answered within forty-eight hours.

Great. That means you will lose all the information you just spent fifteen minutes typing in.

You don't click the send button yet.

You leave the screen open.

You try calling again. Reminder: make sure your cell phone is fully charged before beginning the call.

Have you noticed there is never a prompt for exactly what you need?

You start keeping track of the possible presses for your situation but feel the need to keep listening out of fear a better choice is around the corner.

Now you have numbers two, four, seven, and eleven jotted down as possible presses for your issue. Wait. You forget which one is which. You can't begin to start over. Now you just start intensely banging the zero over and over. Sometimes that works, but not this time.

"I am happy to connect you with someone after you provide me with enough information to properly direct your call," says the computer voice. I hate her.

I think every company's telephone system message should begin something like this:

"We will assume you aren't calling us to tell us how wonderful everything went, so

Press one if you have a complaint.

Press two if you received damaged goods.

Press three if you have been waiting longer than thirty-two days for your order to arrive.

Press four if you need to return an item because what you received looks nothing like it did on our website".

And it should end with, "We no longer have a prompt to place an order until we free up our staff from processing the calls we receive from one to four."

The best customer service is if the customer doesn't need to call you, doesn't need to talk to you. It just works.
-Jeff Bezos, CEO and Founder, Amazon

"Let me tell you about my fabulous eggplant recipe."

CHAPTER 13

WHY? BECAUSE I DON'T NEED TO KNOW THAT

Everyone has a different way of greeting people. I don't mean people that you know. I mean the people (strangers really) that you have a brief encounter with when you make a purchase.

- I usually start with "Hello" or "How are you today?" I don't really mean "How are you?" It is just a phrase. Why do they take me so literally? Sometimes I hear:
- "Well, I'll be better in forty-two minutes when my shift is done."
- "Freezing. Why can't they turn up the heat in here?"
- "Ready to go home. Must be something in the air. Customers have been really aggressive today."
- "So exhausted. People came out of the woodwork today."
- "Great now that you showed up, beautiful."

The latter is just creepy.

Now there are those of you who might suggest a couple are legitimate complaints. But please tell me you agree with the fact that they needn't be shared with the customers.

Cashiers in grocery stores can be really chatty. I think they look down the conveyor belt to plan out their conversation strategy based on the number of items and the approximate time you two will be standing across from each other.

Here is what the cashier is thinking:

She has twelve to fifteen items. I have time to tell her about my recent knee surgery.

She has twenty to twenty-five items. I have time to tell her about my recent knee surgery and my dog's newest trick.

She has her entire inventory of items needed for her Thanksgiving feast. I have time to tell her about my recent knee surgery, my dog's newest trick, and my daughter's poor choice for a boyfriend, and then I will ask her what she plans to do with the sweet potatoes.

I'm happy to share my recipes, and I love dog tricks. But keep the personal dirty laundry out of the chitchat!

As uncomfortable as that can get, it certainly is better than when you begin your checkout and the cashier and bagger are so engrossed in their own personal conversation that you might as well be invisible. Hello, ladies. You are working now, and I am standing here.

And they continue chatting throughout your checkout, except for an offhand "thank you" as you exit the aisle.

Did they not know they would be working with customers? Would they prefer the clientele stay home?

Do you think there was a segment of their training program on tactics to ignore the customers?

Let's make a pact. Let's all start interjecting our thoughts on what they are discussing, and let's make ridiculously off-color remarks and record their reaction. It seems like good material for the next book.

"I'll go get the pillows and blankets from the car."

CHAPTER 14

WHY? BECAUSE IT SHOULDN'T TAKE SO LONG

How about the DMV operation? I know. You're rolling your eyes, aren't you? Oh, yes, another government-run venture. Again, I know it's not a "business," but we still deserve to be treated pleasantly and have the process conducted efficiently, agreed?

I wonder if the higher-ups in Washington have to go there or if they have "people" to go for them.

It is not so painful for emissions testing and license renewal, but if you move across state lines and require new plates and licenses, you'd best be armed with a cooler and a sleeping bag. We have moved multiple times so we have done this process on several occasions.

We take a day off from work. You have to. We arrive as soon as the doors open. We begin the "get a number and take a seat" corralling. It's the same drill. On numerous times you are sent to the next step to "take a number and have a seat."

You pray that you read the instructions thoroughly and have all the required paperwork. God help you if you have to start over on a different day.

Phew! We made it through the first step of paper review.

We moved to the next section to "take a number and have a seat." We waited so long that we have exhausted all of the items on my list that I needed to discuss with my husband regarding this move.

Phew! We made it through the second step.

We moved to the next section to "take a number and have a seat."

How can this be? We are numbers ninety-two and ninety-three, and they are only at forty-seven on the number board. There aren't even that many people waiting to add up to the forty-five numbers between ours and the screen. Did someone think it would be funny to pull all those numbers out and make the employees call out to no one forty-five times?

We have a seat and wait and wait. It's been at least twenty minutes, and the number board is only at fifty. And still barely anyone is sitting in this section.

I decided to ask. I tell my husband, "Do not move a muscle. Keep your eyes peeled on the number board. It might just be stuck and suddenly jump to ninety-two."

The employee asked where I was sitting and which stations I had completed thus far. I proudly told her, "We are waiting for step three."

You have to be kidding! It turned out we were holding numbers for step three but were sitting in the section for step four. Shouldn't they do something to better define where to sit for each step?

I rushed back to gather up our things and find a seat in the step three section.

Oh no! We looked at the number board and see we missed our turn. They are on ninety-six. Surely they would allow us to jump right in to the next available window.

Of course not. "Sorry, but you need to take a new number and have a seat" was the unemotional robotic response I got.

Again we waited. Now my husband and I had time to decide where to go on vacation and even booked the flights online, and you all know how long that takes!

Finally it was our turn at two adjacent windows. I heard my husband turn on the drippingly sweet chitchat in his French accent. He was not yet an American citizen but a legal alien, and we stressed over ensuring we had all the necessary paperwork for him to go through the process. He couldn't possibly take another day off!

I saw what he was doing. The sly dog was going to charm his way through this step. That way she wouldn't notice that all his papers were in French. What did she care anyway? She barely spoke English herself.

And where had my gal gone with all my papers?

Just as my husband was getting up and singing "Thank you very much, ma'am!" I was told that my copy of my birth record would not be sufficient.

Was this a cruel joke? The Frenchman was moving on to the picture stage, and I had to come back? Not that I wanted to jinx his good fortune, but I had to bite my tongue to not yell out, "You just let him through with papers in French that no one could read and my copy from an upstanding town office in Millinocket, Maine, is not good enough?"

I barely spoke to him on the way home as I made phone calls to my hometown to find someone who could get me what I needed to spend another sunshiny day at the DMV.

Seriously it shouldn't be this hard, people.

"And I hate this song."

CHAPTER 15
WHY? BECAUSE IT IS TOO MUCH INFORMATION

Why do some companies have so much detail on their message answering devices? It is so annoying to have to listen to all of that. They need training on how to output just the necessary facts.

One of the doctors we use has a two-minute and fifty-four-second narrative before you can leave a message. Let's just call it three minutes. That's longer than it takes to make a soft-boiled egg, for goodness sake. Specifically:

1. The message reminds us of the name of the practice and then names every doctor in the practice individually. Luckily it leaves out their heights and weights.

2. It tells us what to do for a life-threatening emergency, which is dragged out and emphasized, something like "LLLIFFFE."

3. It tells us what to do for urgent medical issues that are not "LLLIFFFE" threatening, including how to leave a message, what to include, what to do if the doctor hasn't called back within thirty minutes, and so forth.

4. It then lists every staff member's name, extension to reach them, and every possible issue you might have to be connected to them.

Finally I think it will beep and I can leave my message. There's no beep. I wait. Suddenly another voice, different from the first, comes on. And no kidding, people. She repeats the entire litany of instructions that the first half of the message already gave me.

Do they have a secret desire to do voiceovers?

Step by step, every detail is repeated, including the emphasis on "**LLLIFFFE.**"

At the end of her chronicle, finally I hear a beep, and I look down. And as I mentioned, my phone notes two minutes and fifty-four seconds as the time on the call.

By now, I am so exhausted that I don't remember why I called. Oh yeah, I want health forms for the kids' schools.

I think any answering machine message over thirty seconds is just narcissistic.

I have a suggestion. I recommend they spend less time scripting their phone message, which would free them up to spend more time researching manufacturers of examination apparel. Why can't they come up with a more stylish gown? Really now, do they have to be so unattractive or, worse still, made of a crunchy paper material?

Unfortunately it is not just this doctor's office, but most businesses are extending the greeting message with multiple instructions to spend less time actually talking to us. Sad but true.

While we are on doctors' offices, have you noticed that going to a doctor's appointment has become similar to going to the DMV? It has gotten to the point where you need to take a day off because they make you wait sooooo long.

I try to book for either the first appointment of the morning or right after lunch. But that doesn't always work either.

You try showing up early to maybe get in a bit ahead of your booked time. But you hear, "I'm sorry, but your appointment isn't scheduled for another half hour so you will just have to wait."

You try to show up just on time. But you hear, "Just to let you know, the doctor is running thirty minutes behind schedule today."

You dare to show up late. But you hear, "I'm sorry, but your appointment was for fifteen minutes ago. You will need to reschedule because we can't possibly squeeze you in."

This just isn't fair.

On occasion, I've waited so long that, by the time I get in the examination room, my fuming has made my blood pressure readings soar. This then leads to an immediate emergency room referral.

"No need!" I want to scream out. "It's all your fault."

Do they go through this when they have doctor visits? Maybe there is a Doctor's Guild precedent, "We are a busy brotherhood. Never keep another doctor waiting for his or her appointment."

I want to join that clan.

Here is an idea for what would be a very popular company benefit: paid days off for doctor visits to prevent taking sick days.

I like it.

"Fly, my little pins. Fly!"

CHAPTER 16
WHY? BECAUSE IT ISN'T LOGICAL

Am I the only one who goes to pick up an article of clothing that was altered, only to have it suddenly be too small? How can that happen? When I took it in, it was huge. The seamstress had all the pins in the right places.

I pricked myself in several spots while I strategically took it off after she measured me, and the pins were still intact right where she placed them.

I am picturing an evil alterations fairy flying around the shop after they close, moving all the pins. What other explanation can there be?

Recently I took my daughter to have a school skirt hemmed, telling them,

"School guidelines require no more than three inches above the knee."

We spend way too much time measuring my daughter's kneecap to ensure we met guidelines while getting the skirt as short as she possibly desired. *Was I trying to have all articles of clothing be no larger than a washcloth when I was her age?* I pondered through this argument.

After the seamstress marked the spot with a pin and we all agree, I suggested she tell me the total length of the skirt so I could bring in two others and not need to have my daughter in attendance, thus avoiding the heated negotiations of the skirt length in the future.

She told me eighteen inches total length and

twenty-five-inch waist, which I quickly recorded in my phone for future reference.

Imagine our surprise a week later when we picked up the altered skirt, got it home, and tried it on. You could almost see parts that no parent wants exposed. I got out my tape measure.

"The skirt is fifteen and three-quarters end to end, and she cut off all the extra hem material that could make it longer!" I shrieked.

I am telling you, folks. Something must be moving pins at night.

Much to my daughter's embarrassment, we went back, and they did find a way to hem again to the proper length, but here is the kicker. Now we could see the previous stitch holes, and the first ironed hemline was visible along the bottom. No one offered an apology at any point.

Hey, she has a skirt for school, but when are mistakes going to be accompanied with an "I'm sorry ... Sorry we got it wrong ... Sorry you had to come back ... Sorry you must now come back again to pick it up after we get it right"?

Can anyone say "I'm sorry" when he or she makes a mistake? I think it would go a long way.

I thought that was the end of the story. On the day my daughter put on the altered/altered again skirt, we discovered, when taking out the hem to make the length longer, the material was cut in two places, and a patch of material was added from underneath and cross-stitched.

We didn't notice these patch jobs when we picked it up because one was in the back and a pleat partially concealed the other. I couldn't believe it! How could they not have mentioned these dreadful repairs?

I made my fifth trip back. My daughter refused to

come with me to avoid further embarrassment with my persistence. I was calm as a cucumber, but I laid it all out as if I were screaming.

Oh, I wanted to raise my voice and give them a piece of my mind, no surprise to my children who have brought out this side of me on many occasions. It was hard to hold back, but it made for a successful outcome. They paid for a new skirt and gave us free alterations. I felt it was a fair deal, but I did let the ladies know that I would be back to relay the entire story to the owner so they'd best tell him first.

I think they are still sweating a little.

I have since patronized this shop with dry cleaning. Can I tell you that the cashier and tailor smile brightly and have an overly kind and solicitous demeanor now?

The question remains as to whether their recent behavior is because I spoke up or I mentioned I would make sure their boss knew the details of the mishap. We will never know for sure!

"Shoot. I forgot my hearing aids."

CHAPTER 17
WHY? BECAUSE IT IS FUNNY

This is not an unpleasant service encounter exactly. This is the opposite to pulling the wool over our eyes. In this case, giving us too much information made us (actually my husband) doubt our choices.

For twenty-two years, my husband and I have taken, in my opinion, way too long to make decisions. Finding a new home takes forever to the point where the kids need to start school and we have to scramble for a rental. Buying a new lawn mower when ours breaks down takes so much research that I need to hire an interim company to mow so we don't have to harvest hay. Appliances must be totally broken and repair attempts exhausted before we can begin to think of looking for a replacement.

Then a search process commences.

Some of this thoughtful due diligence is good training for the kids, but at some point, I feel like it borders on abuse, for me in particular since I am charged with the investigation and providing the rationale for why we need something. My suggestions for replacement options to consider are then highly scrutinized. This is getting old for me!

Left to my own devices, I can pick out a new couch in less than an hour and choose wall color in ten minutes flat. What is the point of mulling and discussing for so long? As the expression goes, nothing is certain except death and taxes. We can learn from our mistakes and do it differently next time around if necessary, right?

I have long encouraged my husband to get a decent car. The entire time I have been with him, he drove his beloved rusted-out 1983 Jeep and then took my old SUV when I got the new SUV to drive. After all, we have kids, and he wanted us to be safe.

He has had a dream of one day owning a sports car, and I encouraged him. I hate to drive up beside a nice car and see an elderly man hunched over inside. "Get it while you can still sit up nice and straight," I egged on.

He had been looking for this perfect car for over a year now. He just couldn't seem to make up his mind. This also involved me accompanying him on several trips to dealerships. I saw friends for dinner during the exhausting process, and they suggested I need to subliminally help him choose. They obviously don't know him as well as I do. Like all of our previous big-ticket decisions, I was going to have to physically steer him to one model and push him in.

Hallelujah, the day had come, and he finally knew what he wanted. I happily agreed to tag along, as I just wanted to get it over with. *Please God, could he choose and let us stop talking about this purchase?* I thought.

We pulled up to the dealership, and everyone was so cordial. It was bottled waters all around for the group.

The sales manager was so happy to see him. After all, he and my husband had an email romance going on for over a year, and I was sure he had lost all hope of ever actually meeting my husband.

My husband immediately knew which one he wanted. I said, "Beautiful choice. Let's pick our colors." And we were off and running.

Suddenly the human resource professional in me kicked in. "Why should we buy this style versus all the others we have been considering?" I quizzed him.

He retorted, "I am not a pushy salesman, but I think this product is the best. That is why you are here." I silently agreed he didn't need to have a convincing sales pitch because, if you have chosen to walk through those doors, you know you want to be there.

One thing led to another, and I could see the light at the end of the tunnel: colors, extras, payment plans, and such. Suddenly the conversation went to tires. Because it's a sports car, I think many would use their purchase on fair-weather outings but would have a backup vehicle for nasty, wintery weather. That, however, was not my husband's intention. This was to be his daily transportation.

"You will pop tires," the manager bluntly told us.

"How often?" my husband asked.

"Once every couple of months," he answered so matter-of-factly.

I looked at my husband's face and watched it turn an ashen color, which said to me, *Here we go again. He is doubting his decision.*

The manager continued, "I suggest a tire/rim insurance to cover replacements for three years for two thousand dollars.

"Sounds fair, and that program is a must," I hurriedly came back with.

We discussed their service requirements. Oh, lucky us. They had another program for two thousand dollars, which covered us for three years of service at a 30 percent savings.

I looked at my husband, and I knew we were losing him.

He was staring blankly, and I knew what he was thinking, *I have made a big mistake in coming here.*

So I jumped right in, "That sounds like a great deal, doesn't it, dear?"

There was an awkward moment of silence. Suddenly my husband spoke, "Since you are being so honest with us today, is there anything else besides the fragile tires that I need to know about?"

"Well, yes," replied the manager. "You need to start the engine every couple days, or the battery dies."

At this point, the hubby's eyebrows were raised so high that they almost met his hairline.

"Are you telling me, if I don't use the car over the weekend, it won't start on Monday morning?" my husband posed.

Now I lost it totally. I started laughing so hard that I really should have been wearing Depends. I couldn't stop. This was truly a scene from a sitcom.

Once again, the manager had a solution. "Well, we recommend this charger system that plugs into the trunk and also into an outlet in your garage."

"Let me guess," my husband responded. "That will be two thousand dollars also?"

I knew my husband was about to suggest that we best be leaving (without a car), and I couldn't bear to begin this search process with him again. So I emphatically assured him it would not be a big deal to plug that in.

"What if I forget?" he posed to me because he knows himself.

My response to this would typically be, "You just have to remember for yourself. I am already remembering everything for three humans, plus a monthly heartworm and tick application for the dog."

But not this time. I could not let this be the deal breaker. "I'll help remind you, honey," I assured him as sincerely as if I had my hand on a Bible at that moment.

We signed the papers, and the rest is history.

I guess the moral is that we consumers won't be deterred, even with an extremely honest salesperson, if we are unwavering in our goal. Although we had different motivations, both of us wanted to get a car. I see it as a win-win, so to speak.

Now we can begin the search for a new indoor/outdoor thermometer. I hope to have that wrapped up within six months.

Wish me luck.

CHAPTER 18

WHY NOT? BECAUSE IT IS ITS OWN BOOK

Can you bear to read a chapter on the perils of working with any of the construction and building trades?

Me neither. Now there is a special category of *professionals*. An entire book can be devoted to their antics.

I would say that 97.2 percent of our encounters with them are horrendous or outlandish.

And there's the end of that story.

"Looks good, fellas."

CHAPTER 19
WHY? BECAUSE EITHER WAY WE PAY

Here is an interesting question: do educational institutions need to be concerned with service? After all, if we are referring to the public school arena, our taxes fund them. And if the question is posed as it relates to the private school systems, again we pay.

Don't some interactions with them make you feel as if it were our privilege that they are educating our children? For sure they can have unrealistic demands from a myriad of helicopter parents, but I presume this is a minority parent category. Perhaps this group exacerbates a defensive reaction among educators, resulting in them having their guard up a fair amount of the time. "Prepare for the parent who finds everything wrong at the school. Do everything just short of asking him or her to find another educational facility," might be advice given in their opening day meeting speech. I don't know.

We all start out each year optimistically. We assume teachers will treat all fairly and distribute their devotion equally. Sometimes it works out, but human nature being what it is, not always. It is too bad when teachers form favorites. I imagine it can sometimes be difficult not to gravitate to the students who sit quietly in their seats and diligently do their work. It's a difficult act, one I could never do, but the teachers who have the ability to balance and inspire should be paid significant salaries.

One theory that will assist to support an upgrade of the educational experience would be to implement professional employee review systems, like good business practices that the public sector has to conduct. They don't always work seamlessly, but when supported by top management, it is an invaluable annual tool to development people.

Probably that idealistic notion will take a long time, if ever, because most educational institutions currently have minimal processes in place.

Is there anyone in alignment with me? I am quite opposed to tenured positions, particularly in education. It diminishes incentives to strive for greatness and fosters mediocrity.

I realized, similar to a previous chapter on seniors' benefits, I just can't seem to make it funny. I now figured out why. Taking care of the older generation and providing a solid education to all children are really serious matters. These are two initiatives that still need some work in our country.

I just decided to donate some of the profits from this book to a nonprofit whose mission is devoted to children's education.

I don't know yet whom that will be, but I will do my due diligence.

Stay tuned.

If you don't genuinely like your customers,
chances are they won't buy.
—Tom Watson, IBM CEO

"One eye, okay. No legs, defective.
No mouth, okay ... ..."

CHAPTER 20

WHY? BECAUSE THERE IS NO RATIONALE FOR THIS

Is it my imagination, or does there seem to be an escalation in recalls: food and drug products, furniture items, and manufacturing snafus? What is going on with that?

At first I theorized that someone at the top was not involved enough in what was going on. But now I have an additional theory. Might it be that someone in mid-management took a shortcut? Obviously someone in the management chain is not paying close enough attention.

I do believe that top management is sometimes surprised when they learn of these mishaps. However, they are in charge, correct? God help us if they are trying to cover errors for fear of their top line.

Someone in the upper ranks is not actively involved enough in what is going on with someone down the management ranks.

Everyone in a company has to stay involved in the functionality and day-to-day operation of the area he or she is responsible for. It is the only way to minimize mistakes and ensure things continue to run smoothly. When mistakes happen, they need to be corrected quickly and efficiently, and an organization needs to learn from them.

Remember the "heart of the house" stories? Everyone

must be trained to understand how important his or her individual function is to the final output. Also the work environment must be one that allows for honesty without fear of retribution. That would only make employees fearful to point out defects. It is best to catch deficiencies as early as possible.

And let me ask you: do you agree with the notion that a company can have various levels of imperfections? I take liberty here from a company policy recently exposed. As my illustration humorously points out, items that register defect levels one through three will pass and continue through production. Defect levels four through six need a further look. Give me a break. Defects are defects and demand a correction in processes or procedures.

I think, as consumers, when we placidly accept recalls, we have given up the good fight and resigned ourselves to expect flaws. Let's not. Let's continue to speak up.

Unfortunately recalls are becoming so commonplace that it has been a great venue for me to use for April Fool's pranks. Last year I cooked up one of my best. I got my friend Tom (thank you, Tom!) to call my parents and tell them there was a recall on their brand-new car, which my stepfather had spent months researching as "the best new vehicle on the entire planet," according to him. They are in their eighties. My mother got diarrhea stressing over the bad choice they had made.

Okay, I 'fessed up when she was freaking out, but they have pulled some doozies on me over the years as well.

Recalls give me fodder.

IT CAN BE DONE

"Where is my password book?"

CHAPTER 21

WHY? BECAUSE IT IS LESS FRUSTRATING

I hate to admit this. My retail career put a roof over my head for twenty-three years, but for the last two holiday seasons, I abandoned them and ordered every present online. That's right, people. I never entered a store from November 15 until January 5.

"Why?" you might ask.

Too crowded.

No one to help you.

If they hired Christmas extras, they are inadequately trained.

Parking is a nightmare. I could reply.

And I could go on.

So I sit at my cozy desk with a piping hot cocoa and order away. Now don't think that process goes so smoothly either. Repetitively filling out your name, address, and payment choices gets old. Yes, of course you can register, create a password, and eliminate that step for the next order placement, but do you want to?

That comes with another whole host of problems, starting with the fact that now you need a book in which to keep all the usernames and passwords. Of course, no two companies have similar requirements for creating usernames and passwords.

Each company calls for different guidelines:

- No uppercase
- One uppercase
- Four numbers and five letters
- No symbol
- Two letters, two symbols, and six numbers

Literally speaking, our house has a notebook dedicated to this library of codes. I try to use the same username and password for as many as I can to cut down on the confusion, but usually it doesn't meet what the website requires. Then it becomes the question, "Did I use my old standby codes for this company, or is this one where I had to come up with something different?"

Thus, the codebook has saved us all in this family, unless of course the kids take the book to find a code and then can't remember where they left it. That happened last year. It is a wonder they are still allowed to live with us after what we went through to re-create years of ingenious password phrases.

And what about when you don't want to register? You just want to add your item to your cart, pay, and have your items sent. It is so annoying when you miss the fact that, during your checkout, the box was already checked for future emails, notifications of sales events, advertising, and so forth from this site.

I miss unchecking the box frequently, so then I spend most of January unsubscribing from the very tiny option at the very bottom of their emails. I am back to regular email flow by March usually.

Please listen up, online stores. Kindly leave the box un-checked and let us make up our own minds about whether we want all that extra email traffic or not.

"I wonder if I have time to get a coffee."

CHAPTER 22

WHY? BECAUSE THEIR FUNCTION IS QUESTIONABLE

I think the insurance brokerage/agent industry is an interesting study. What is their function exactly?

After the initial sign-up, the most communication you get from the agent are renewal notices and notifications of plan changes. Even the annual premium bill comes directly from the carrier.

On the couple of instances when we have had a claim, they basically gave us the telephone number for the claims department at the insurance company to work with us.

Wouldn't it be nice if they made that call? Don't you think they could drive the dented vehicle to the body repair shop for the estimate for us? Well, maybe we drive it for the estimate, but then they drive it for the approved repair. The process always means two trips. Let's split them.

Why don't they find me a tree/fence company to repair damages from a fallen tree? They could just tell me what the cost will be from their competitive shopping. Why do I have to do all the work? And why don't they call in the estimate to the insurance claims department? I don't get it.

My husband had to ask for a review of policies and potential new carrier choices. If he hadn't taken the initiative, I fear we would have just carried on status quo until we moved to an assisted living community.

And guess what the review produced? Good reasons for a move to a new insurance carrier.

Why don't the brokerage offices do reviews on a regular basis? Oh, wait. That would be great, not just adequate service. What a novel idea.

We were rear-ended twice last winter, both times by the same car make and model. If I see one coming now, I pull off into the nearest ditch. Anyway, by the second accident, we were already with the new carrier.

What a difference! I barely had to do anything. By the way, the agent still did nothing, but I guess I can be thankful that she recommended this efficient, customer-oriented new insurance find.

My fear is that some huge conglomerate will swoop in and acquire them to beef up their portfolio offerings and things will start to go south.

I hope not.

The customer's perception is your reality.
**–Kate Zabriskie, president,
Business Training Works**

"Oh, look! There she blows!!"

CHAPTER 23

WHY? BECAUSE THEIR VERY BEING MAKES FOR GOOD STORIES

By now you have discerned that I am perpetually miffed at the repeated dysfunction by various branches of the government. I know I have already mentioned a few examples, but their breach of efficiency is so far-reaching and affects all of us every day, even down the chain to the local municipality governments. This scenario is a clear case in point, mingled with some other problematic service philosophies.

Last summer I booked a four-hour whale watch for the kids and their visiting cousins. There was chaotic excitement for the excursion and such anticipation in the car ride there. We were hoping to check in early to get prime viewing seats for the trip.

Parking in this vacation town is difficult, and the maximum parking time limit that I could find was a three-hour lot.

How can a town offer a four-hour boat ride and only have one-, two-, or three-hour parking all around the departure area? I thought.

Oh well. We'd miss the boat if I didn't just pick something soon, but at least I would save time because I bought the tickets online. So I took a chance in the closest three-hour lot. We would be illegal for only one hour, and my time of entry would only be noticed if the ticket police were in the lot right then to chalk my tire. I didn't see any men in blue in the lot, so we parked and ran.

"Hurry, kids. We don't want to miss the boat. I'm so glad I bought the tickets online to save time," I said.

"But wait," a young man standing next to the cashier stations told me as I tried to sail past the fifty-plus people waiting in line for the *two* open ticket booth operators. (Yes, I counted. Seven window stations yet only two humans manning two open booths.) "You must also get in line to get printed tickets."

What the heck is the paper I hold in my hand with a scannable bar code that clearly states I have just purchased five tickets for the whale watch at eight thirty in the morning on June 14? I thought.

"That just holds your reservation," the young man proclaimed, giving off the impression that his sole purpose was to guard the two gals printing tickets and taking payments.

What is his function anyway? I thought. *Why the heck doesn't he open up an additional cashier window and get this line moving?*

We waited. Well, I waited while the four kids roamed around. It was now eight twenty. The line was made up of people for three different cruises. Ours departed in ten minutes for whale watching. A sightseeing boat was leaving at nine thirty, and a lighthouse tour was scheduled for ten thirty.

Why don't they make an announcement for people going on the later two trips to please step to the side so the eight thirty whale watch patrons don't miss the boat?

I always have sound logical questions. Why can't anyone give me sound logical answers?

We made it, but not because we jumped the line. They held the boat until eight forty-five when everyone had gotten their tickets and was safely on board.

That is a ridiculous way to handle it, if you ask me. Schedule more cashiers based on multiple boat departure demands. And when in a pinch, move groups through by boat departure times.

Isn't that logical to you?

Well there, I thought to myself, *things should go smoothly from here on out.*

But as I handed the five paper tickets (which I waited in line for) to the boat hand, he warned us, even though it was a beautiful day, yesterday's storms were still producing a significant chop in the open ocean.

"How much?" I asked.

"Four- to five-foot swells," he warned.

"No biggie for this group," I assured him. "They have been deep sea fishing for years. Very far out. Right, kids?"

They all nodded.

Well, it was fine for us, but everyone on all sides of us started heaving about a half hour into the trip. The boat had brought along five or six extra crew members who were walking around in red coats and hospital gloves. Each had a roll of paper towels under one arm and a sack of barf bags in the other. It seemed their only purpose was to assist those who were spilling their guts. What a fun job they have.

"Kids, stop watching the people getting sick. It will make you sick also," I suggested to my four.

What a scene! People were running for wastebaskets or, better yet, trying to get outside in the fresh air.

"Kids, don't look, please," I was begging them now.

Meanwhile on the upper deck, the naturalist was talking nonstop, enthusiastically pointing out every possible bird, seal, and puffin along the way. When we happened to be in an area with nothing to see, he just started rattling off facts and figures about anything involving nature.

*Does he have any clue of the hospital ward situation be-
low him? Can't he look down from his post and see the outer
balconies are lined with people wrenching with their bodies
extended over the rail and that pancakes and scrambled eggs
barely eaten an hour before are flying through the sea air?*

Now the naturalist made an announcement, "There
doesn't seem to be any whales in our usual spots, folks. The
captain and I would hate it if you didn't get to see these
majestic giants, so the captain has agreed to continue our
trip further out, just thirty miles off the coast of Nova
Scotia, where we have been told there have been many
sightings. It will take us at least another hour to get there,
so sit back and enjoy the ride."

Is he kidding? Why doesn't he take a vote? I thought.
This isn't democracy in any form of the word.

I could suddenly relate to how any healthy pilgrim must
have felt during the long trip to Plymouth Rock.

Oh no! One of the cousins was turning gray. *Here she
blows! Great! All over my hand.*

"You three kids get outside immediately," I instructed.
"Breathe in the air, and don't tell me it is too cold out there.
I can only hold one bag for one person at a time."

Well, we arrived at the international demarcation, and
just short of needing our passports, we followed two whales
for another forty minutes. Finally the crew was satisfied
that we got our money's worth, so we began the trip home.

I looked at my watch and determined my car would now
have been parked for almost six hours by the time we re-
turned to port.

I strategized my argument.

It was all planned out in my head if I had been issued

a ticket. "Is it my fault that the captain and naturalist decided to take us to Canada?"

The funny thing about seasickness, the minute most get back on solid ground, the feeling is gone, just like my niece who ate the biggest bowl of pasta I ever saw. But I still insisted she hold a bag for the car ride home, just in case.

Of course I got a ticket. We were all so exhausted from the trip that I decided to deal with the ticket another time. About a week later, I made the trip to the police station with the ticket in my hand.

"Are you here to pay for that ticket?" assumed the lady behind the window of glass.

"Not exactly," I said. "I actually wanted to share the tale of why I was parked there for six hours and also to suggest some thought be given to extended time in some of the town lots to accommodate long boat trips.

She rolled her eyes in disgust at the mention of the whole whale watch/sightseeing operation.

Wait a minute, I thought. Don't those trips bring multitudes of people to the town, who then shop and dine before and after the trips? Do you think the town manager would agree with her disdain?

I got nowhere with her, and she sent another "official" over to the window, but I could see it was useless. I stopped trying to justify and asked how much I owed for the ticket.

While I was paying, she offered a suggestion, "Next time, just bring it in and pay for it and put it back on the dash. It is like all-day parking." She was deadpan serious.

This was absurd. How is paying for a ticket the same as all-day parking?

I have it. Maybe there should be a sign as you enter the lot.

This is an all-day lot.
If you stay parked for over three hours, you get a ticket.
Come to the police station and pay for it.
But come on foot so you don't lose your parking spot.
After that, walk back and place paid ticket on dashboard
to alert next parking cop that you already paid.
You are all set for a day of fun.
Thank you for visiting us!

Unbelievable, isn't it? It's another example of people in authority not walking in our shoes to experience what they ask us to walk. Get your sneakers on, folks.

"It seems we are supposed to swim back."

"Who determines the placement of these things?"

CHAPTER 24

WHY? BECAUSE THEY PROVIDE LOTS OF MATERIAL

So you are travelling and will be staying in an establishment that you will be calling "home sweet home" for the time you are away. Be it motel, hotel, inn, or B&B, it will be your place to sleep, shower, dress, dine, drink, and relax.

I probably could be diagnosed with OCD if I were tested, but I can't help but be a bit freaked out when I first open the door to my temporary abode. Immediately questions start going through my head.

Exactly who was here before me?

What did they do in this room?

Now I am picturing someone rush from the shower and sit naked at the desk chair to jot down notes before he or she forgets his or her thoughts.

Did any feet that tiptoed across this carpet have a severe case of athlete's foot? I have to force myself to stop my imagination from running further to prevent me from contemplating a night spent sleeping in the car.

I always request a nonsmoking room. Have you ever entered a room and are willing to bet one hundred dollars that they just made it a nonsmoking room that morning? That bugs me.

You already know the room was not vacuumed well when you find a nickel on the rug. Could the operations department purchase vacuum machines with attachments that actually get into the corners? I have seen some totally unrecognizable piles of stuff in the corners. Those huge industrial machines they use are perfect for the long, straight hallways, but not for corners.

I highly recommend every establishment post a visible checklist in the room. You know, like the elevator inspections where we can actually see a date of when it was last tested and serviced.

Here are some examples:
- Comforter was dry cleaned on _____
- Carpet was shampooed on _____
- Furniture was upholstered on _____

This would make me feel better.

For sure, functionally minded individuals are not involved in the room design. What is in a standard room? You can expect to have a bed, one or two nightstands, and a bureau that is three-fifths useless, by the way, as it only has two drawers available. Half of it is disguised to hold a mini refrigerator, and the top drawer displays snacks for sale as well as the TV remotes. Then there is a desk the size of my kitchen table with a desk chair. Finally, if you are lucky, there might be room left over for an upholstered chair that comfortably sits anyone *under* the age of twelve.

I get having a desk. If you are traveling for business, you probably need one, but it would be just as functional at half the size. And let me ask you: have you actually found any available outlets near the desk to charge your laptop and phone?

Exactly. After you have crawled around and under the desk searching, you resort to utilizing the bathroom outlets. Now your vanity is clogged with your charging devices.

And for the million other reasons we stay in a place, other than our own bed, how much is the desk actually utilized? Do you plan to sit there frequently if you are honeymooning in St. Lucia? Are the kids begging you for a homework space while you are on spring break?

I deduce that many lodgings assume we will just sit on the bed. It is too awkward to sit on a bed. There are three ways to position yourself:

1. You sit with your feet squarely on the floor, but this means your head is cranked at a ninety-degree angle to view TV.
2. You try swinging your feet up on the bed and propping pillows behind your back to make it feel like you are in a chair with a footrest.
3. Or you lay fully prone, and now you are not sitting at al. Now you are sleeping.

So if the desk were not sized to sit six people, there might be room for a comfy club chair. I would definitely consider lounging there, after I verified from the checklist that it was recently upholstered, of course.

Also in the room is a closet. It's so inefficient with one closet designed for all hanging items with one shelf above. Who travels with five feet of hanging clothes? Most of us have some hanging items, but the rest is folded and needs shelves. The shelf in the closet is already taken up with pillows and an iron. As mentioned, the bureau really exists for other purposes. So where are we supposed to put the folded shirts, shorts, jammies, and unmentionables? On the floor?

Then there is a bathroom. I have seen such a range from the small, minimalist style with just a freestanding sink that can't hold a toothbrush, let alone any other toiletries, to the expansive vanity top (in the same establishments with the dining room-sized desks) that I spend the first ten minutes clearing off water glasses, ring dish, potpourri bowls, and booklets for the spa and shopping in order to make some space to place my things.

I have another question. Can someone devote time to a thorough analysis of hair dryers? I've had all extremes from the low-wattage type that only dries one hair at a time to the models that actually singe your ends. Isn't there a happy medium? Regarding those wall unit dryers, who decided to make them with just five inches of cord? You can't even get back in front of the mirror to see yourself when you are using it.

Vow to self: I promise to forgo packing one fabulous pair of shoes to make room in my suitcase for my professional-grade dryer from this day forward.

Why do they have scales in the bathrooms? They want us to spend money in their lounges and dining rooms by indulging to excess, so why do they want us to hate ourselves in the morning? Scales are for doctors' offices and home. Period.

No matter your room rate, by the way, no one should have tattered sheets or towels. Who could possibly continue to make up a bed with a sheet that is frayed on the edge? How could the housekeeper miss the fact that she left me with a stained bath towel and a washcloth with a hole in the middle?

I find, 90 percent of the time, at least one thing is wrong that requires me to call the front desk. The tub drain is broken. The register is blowing cold air on a twenty-two-degree day. The room is missing a hair dryer. (Even if it burns me, I still need one.) But the frequent call is for replacement light bulbs. Do they follow a checklist, or do they prefer to wait until they get a call from the room occupant? Is it their philosophy that it takes less time to respond to a complaint than to have the housekeeping team test them during their rounds?

How about the complicated bedside "clock"? I think some of them might even give massages if you can figure out how to give them the proper command. I am going to start traveling with a mechanical engineer on my future trips to set up the clock for me. Or maybe it is time I learned how the alarm on my phone actually functions. Surely that would be the easier approach for a simpleton like me.

Many establishments now offer a coffee setup in the room. It usually takes me twenty minutes to figure out how to operate the thing and find everything I need to make a cup of coffee. Instructions might be helpful, people.

I don't really like any version of milk that isn't in a liquid state, but when in a pinch, I surrender to the powdered stuff.

So you have made your coffee, and now you have some debris: a used stirrer, sugar packet, and an empty dried "milk" container to throw away.

Have you noticed that there isn't a wastebasket within a half-mile radius of the coffee setup?

You start to walk around the room, balancing the throw-aways in your hands. Oops, you drop something. Oh darn. A little bit of sugar was left inside the packet, and now it is on the carpet. Gosh, that stirrer held a drop of coffee on the end and just landed on my beige skirt.

Just give us a wastebasket near the coffee setup, please.

Can someone think functional here?

I think I will put myself out for hire after the book.

My title will be DSLFD, director of sensible logistics and functional design.

Being on par in terms of price and quality only gets you into the game. Service wins the game.
-Dr. Tony Allesandra, author, motivational speaker

"Please be empty. Please be empty."

CHAPTER 25

WHY? BECAUSE I AM THE DSLFD

So in my new position as director of sensible logistics and functional design, my first project would be to push for reform of all building restroom design. It is just stupid to have a restaurant that seats a hundred people with two stalls for the ladies.

Haven't you noticed that every restaurant, sports arena, theater, and airport has a long line for the ladies' room and no line for the men's room? Do the math. You can fit six urinals in the same square footage as just two stalls.

And never should anyone's knees touch the door, for goodness sake.

Here are a few more questionable doozies:

- Why do the manual car washes only give you fifteen seconds of drying time? Is there anyone out there who has been able to strategically time that drive-thru to get the entire car dried before the machines shut off?
- Why do some clothing stores cram their display racks and four-ways so close together that you have to turn yourself sideways to pass through them?
- How is it possible that a pharmacy can get a refill wrong, specifically one that has been in their system as the same prescription reordered for six years running?

- Why do grocery stores put their freestanding display cases at such an angle in the aisles? If you meet a cart bombing down from the opposite direction, it becomes a battle as to who can pass through the maze first. I am usually quite determined to win that race, unless of course it is an elderly person or a parent with small children. Like the airlines, I always allow them to go first.
- And why do I always seem to get the slow lane to check out? I can be third in my line, and by the time it is my turn, the folks who were seventh or eighth on either side of me in their lanes are also checking out.
- Have you seen how some people walk back and forth to try to determine which will be the fastest line? You can overhear their analysis before deciding which lane to get in, "Okay, I went back and forth twice. There are three people in lanes three and four with about fifteen items each but only one person in lane seven with a full cart. Let's go there so we are next."
- I really don't want to take the time for this assessment to then make my best guess as to which one I choose. Perhaps thought could be given to a system of "arrive first, check out first." I like the stores that have you form a single line. There you get called as cashiers become open. It seems to work pretty well in some of the large retail chains.
- I know nice weather is a necessity for road repair, but wouldn't it make sense to schedule it not at peak hours when millions of drivers hit the roads for some summer fun?
- The final functional design thought to ponder is this question: who the heck is in charge of parking lot

design? Why do the parking space widths have such disparity among lots? Why can't they be more uniform, taking into account all car sizes, including my large SUV? While my husband continues to remind me of all the "functional" reasons we still have a honking tank, all I can keep dreaming about is the joy of having a vehicle that I don't have to squeeze myself out of when getting out. I am tired of catching my shirt on the lock button and having a grease imprint on the back of my clothes from rubbing up against the door opening. And the compact car sections must have been designed for golf carts. Are any of you using a golf cart to get around besides at the golf course?

These are just a few examples. I could go on, and I am sure you could weigh in as well.

Why do I have to point these things out?

I think I am going to be in high demand as the DSLFD.

"Give me my money, damn it."

CHAPTER 26

WHY? BECAUSE MONEY IS THE ROOT

Maybe it is a good thing that banks are progressively becoming more automated, even though I previously complained about the lack of people contact in past chapters. Many number of my interactions over the years have made me consider running away as fast as I could. Maybe I can just put my money under a rock and hope for the best.

Recently on a rare occasion when I actually went into the bank, I was behind a gentleman in line who was making a large deposit with rolled coins, cash, and checks. I spent a long time trying to analyze what kind of business he was in with all of that mixed deposit, but that is beside the point. The real point is that you should have seen the disgruntled look on the teller's face, like she couldn't believe she had to count all that. Isn't that a part of what tellers are hired for? To count money?

Here is a good reason to never have face-to-face contact with bank employees. This is the only story in the book that did not happen to me personally. After my friend told me this tale, I knew it had to go in.

So my friend runs her own consulting firm. Every time she enters her bank branch, one of the managers approaches her to inquire, based on her self-employment, if she might want to consider opening a business line of credit. (Where do they get these kids? Most look like they are seventeen years old.)

She politely declines and attempts to complete her banking business while this youngster continues to rattle off the benefits of opening one.

This same scenario repeats itself each time she goes into the branch to conduct her business. I give her such credit for not causing a scene and screaming, "Stop asking me that!" For sure, I would have yelled that and sought out another branch, even if it meant driving eighteen miles each way. Anything to avoid this annoying sales pitch.

Imagine her surprise one day when in her mail was a letter welcoming her into the business credit line division and thanking her for "entrusting her business needs to them."

Can you believe this story?

Well, she is a good Catholic girl, so I know she is certainly not making this up.

After a lengthy review, with me wondering why it always takes them so long, it was confirmed that the application and her signature had been forged.

Who would do that? I'm betting that manager must be trying to get all the guys to open up checking accounts from his new address in prison now.

Oh, you youngsters don't know what you're in for. Back in the day, banks were happy to have whatever small amounts of money you had tied up at their establishment. You had your simple checking account and a savings account that actually earned interest back then.

When did they start charging for checks?

How dare they eat into my emergency savings account each month because the interest rate doesn't quite cover the cost of their fees and my request for paper statements?

I love it when they suggest you link all your accounts together to avoid fees and then they can't figure out exactly how to do that.

And what are all these levels of "finance managers" they now have? Is it based on how much you have in their system that determines who can talk to you? And what in the world are "private bankers" anyway? Shouldn't all your banking be private?

But as mentioned, banking institutions have done a good job of automating. I have never had an issue online or at an ATM, but it's not so good for my husband. Machines have gobbled up his debit card because he was busy putting the withdrawal in his wallet and evidently didn't take hold of his card fast enough.

Once he didn't grab the money fast enough, and the machine sucked it back in. He did a second transaction. This time he held his hand in front of the slot to not miss his opportunity, and he was successful in pulling out the cash. But this scenario was after hours, so he went back during business hours to straighten it out.

Wouldn't you think it would take one day to read the transaction list and see two three hundred-dollar withdrawals at seven in the morning and then two minutes later and yet the money in the ATM has a three hundred-dollar surplus at the end of the day? It took a four-month review, at which point we received a letter that they were "pleased to report that indeed an error was made and his account would be credited." Ludicrous!

Why has the world of finance become so complex?

There is only one boss. The customer.
And he can fire everybody in the company
from the chairman on down, simply by
spending his money somewhere else.
—Sam Walton, founder, Walmart

"No thanks. I will cut it myself. I only have thirty-six seconds of free parking left."

CHAPTER 27

WHY? BECAUSE THEY NEEDED MENTIONING

I did not even think to add this category of service providers to the list until I went for a haircut recently. Suddenly it dawned on me, "How could I possibly forget them?" Yes, I'm referring to the salons and spas. Now there is money spent on pure indulgence, and every detail should be perfect. We don't really need any of their services, except maybe a haircut now and then, but once in a while, when we have some disposable income, we might like to treat ourselves to a little something.

I go to a salon that has some funky rules. For example, personally I feel like I am wasting precious time if I sit for a blow-dry after getting the roots back to the shade I was a few years ago. I sometimes don't care what I look like as I am leaving the salon, as I am not going anywhere special. But I don't really like the look of the wet hair leaving huge, wet rings on the front and back of whatever shirt I am wearing. Therefore, I like to at least get out the water before walking out onto the street, call it a "mini blow-dry."

Well, in the old days, you could sit at a station and use a dryer to do just that, but now there is a new rule. Evidently some woman (who must not have been quite all there) singed her hair, and just short of a lawsuit, the salon made a ruling that no one could ever dry their own hair again. So you can leave the salon with the aforementioned wet spots, which might mistake you for a woman in dire need of pumping, or you pay fifty-five dollars for someone to blow-dry your hair. And in their mind, style you while they are at it. Do many of us want to add fifty-five dollars to an already-staggering cost of a color job?

The other "service" they have is that you can park in the lot attached to their building and, with their stamp, receive two free hours of parking. I have never gotten out of there in two hours, even if it is just for a haircut. I have gotten to the point where I clearly note the time of entry and monitor my watch throughout my time there to try to beat the clock. It's impossible!

So your color is done, but no shampoo gal is free. Or the shampoo gal, without asking, decides you need a deep scalp conditioning.

Before you know it, the goop is burning your scalp, and she says she can't take it off for fifteen minutes. Or you sail through the color and shampoo, but the stylist is behind schedule.

One time I was actually beating the two-hour time limit with eight minutes to pay, dash for the car, and have the parking be free for once. The cashier decided to answer the ringing phone and proceeded to spend several minutes giving directions to the salon to the caller. Just my luck. No less than seven times, she repeated the salon address, cross street names, parking location, and names of establishments adjacent to, across from, and even behind the salon. Obviously she was talking to someone totally unfamiliar with the area.

You can try to envision the body language and hand signals I used to give her hints to place the caller on hold and cash me out. You can also guess at what came out of my mouth when she finally did hang up. The point is, invariably, I go to hand my ticket to the parking attendant and, for a variety of reasons, I am told I was parked for over two hours and I always owe something. It's maddening!

Is it a prerequisite to be dramatic if you work in this industry? Have you ever met a collective group that has as many personal crises as this profession seems to have? How about the tension you can feel in some shops? They are bickering over who has the bigger manicure station, bemoaning about who has the better chair placement for nabbing walk-ins, complaining that the receptionist never gets any appointments right, and on and on.

Maybe it is the HR in me, but I seem to always bring out the very personal stories of these folks, although that is never my intention. Has this happened to you? They force you to put on your psychologist hat the entire time you are there to counsel them. Hey, this was supposed to be my time!

I am always on time, if not a bit early. I feel people who are late don't really think through how their lack of timeliness affects those around them. Case in point, when someone is late for a salon appointment and the technician accommodates her, and a domino effect takes place. Every client she takes after the turtle puts her off schedule. I think salons should treat it like the doctors' offices. They could say, "Sorry, but you are late. So unless you have an emergency, we can't possibly squeeze you in, and you will have to reschedule." Why should the rest of us wait around when we are on time?

How about the majority of hair cutters who make a big deal of sitting you down for a five-minute verbal analysis of what you are looking for and putting their fingers through your hair to "feel" the texture? And you leave looking nothing like what you envisioned or thought you described. I hate that. This goes back to speaking up because admittedly I don't always. I just look for a new salon. Worse yet, when they get it wrong for one of the kids. You have to listen to their complaining for a month and repeatedly remind them, "It will grow out soon, and we can look for someone else."

I don't know about you, but I refuse to let anyone touch my hair who has green- and blue-striped hair that is shaved over the ear on one side. Have you seen the variety of hairstyles some stylists sport? They must be having a year-round Halloween festival twirling in their head.

One thing is for sure. Once you find a salon technician that you are happy with, you will follow that technician anywhere, even if it means moving to Cuba.

"And these are pictures of Junior each
day of his first year of life."

CHAPTER 28

WHY? BECAUSE IT IS JUST OPEN-MINDED

You know, it is only reasonable to devote one chapter of a book about bad service to discuss obnoxious customers, don't you agree? At best, you have been waiting your turn when you have had the pleasure of witnessing an exchange of this impolite behavior. Or worse yet, you might be one of those joining in on the party.

Let's call them the BBCs
Badly Behaved Consumers

There are the BBCs who conduct their business in slow motion like they are the only people on earth. Are they oblivious to those around them? When I see anyone waiting on me, be it standing in a line, waiting to grab my parking space, or even golfing, I kill myself to vacate so I won't hold up anyone.

Then there are the BBCs who walk up to the person assisting you and blurt out that they just have a "quick" question that ends up taking seven minutes of your cashier's time. How rude is that?

That is similar to the restaurant patron who demands something from just any server passing by his table because he or she is too impatient to wait for his or her own server to surface.

I saw this one time, where the person he flagged down was a fellow diner who was just trying to go to the restroom! He was so obsessed about his own needs that he didn't even notice that the lady was in a red dress while the wait staff were all in black and white.

"Excuse me, could I have more béarnaise sauce?" the man asked while flailing his arm in the air to get her attention.

"I am sure you can. Why don't you ask your server when he comes by?" she coolly replied.

I feel so bad for the staff that has to deal with grumbling BBCs when they are just the middlemen. Take the wait staff at a restaurant. Doesn't that BBC realize the waitress just served the plates and, if the meat was not cooked to their liking, he or she should direct any complaints to the chef?

How about when BBCs are dining in a sit-down restaurant and they send the food back because it came too late? Perhaps they should stick to the drive-thru. Oh, wait. They probably complain there as well.

I once witnessed a lady ream a cosmetic salesperson because the cream she bought gave her a rash. It seemed that this particular salesperson she was screaming at was not even involved in her original visit to purchase it, but she stood there and took it. I felt terrible for her. That is just not called for.

Situations like this sometimes end with the customer threatening, "I won't be back!" I venture to guess that, at least half the time when this is the last statement the salesperson hears, he or she is racing to the back stock-room to pop the bubbly in celebration!

I am mystified when I hear a customer continuing to tell his or her life story to an employee, even though he or she is bagged up, the money was exchanged, and the employee is calling, "Next!"

I waited to pay to exit a parking lot recently for ten minutes, and I was only the second car in line. It turns out the driver ahead of me was yelling at the cashier about how expensive the lot was, like he actually set the rates, for heaven's sake.

Don't get mad at the cashier for prices he can't control. How is he supposed to respond to the BBC comment? Is he supposed to say, "I agree. This is so expensive!" Or could he reply, "So sorry. My apologies." Get real.

That is similar to passengers in the airports screaming at the desk attendant about their delayed flight, like that person single-handedly had the power to delay flight 1932. Or worse, the late flier who is demanding that the door of the plane be reopened even though it has already left the tarmac and is halfway to the runway.

How about the BBCs who can't take the extra twenty-six seconds to return their shopping cart to the designated areas? Worse still, I have seen carts planked right in the middle of the handicapped space. So rude.

I wonder what the employee is thinking while trying to decipher the BBC's hand gestures, because they are ordering while talking on their cell phone at the same time. For heaven's sake, get off the phone and verbalize your order.

And while we are on cell phones, who spends money for a show or concert and misses some of it because he or she is taking and making calls? How about the rest of us who have been assigned the seats around the BBCs?

So it's the age ol' chicken or egg story. Which came first: bad service or badly behaved consumers? Yet another question to ponder, folks.

"We'll watch the baby. You go to the kitchen and find our food."

"Like we need any management tips."

CHAPTER 29
WHY? BECAUSE IT REALLY IS SIMPLE

You know, this book could go on forever. Unfortunately we are programmed to habitually anticipate a situation that might warrant being included as yet another humorous (or scary) tale of poor service. But after a while, the book would be repeating scenarios, sharing common roots to the problem. It really comes down to three significant areas that make the difference:

A. Selection
B. Training
C. Leadership

There you have it, folks. As simple as A, B, and C.

The end. Well, not really. I detail my thoughts on these three crucial components in the epilogue. Feel free to keep reading. There I outline some simple steps to creating a successful service-driven organization.

Warning: there are a few less jokes and sarcasm. It is too important.

I think the next book is going to include names.
Good luck!
Game on, friends.

"Oh, good. He's awake now."

Feedback is the breakfast of champions.
–Ken Blanchard

EPILOGUE

If your actions inspire others to dream more,
learn more, do more, and become more,
you are a Leader.
-President John Quincy Adams

"Note to self: Wash hands as soon
as the interview is over."

THE A CHAPTER

WHY? BECAUSE IT IS ONLY FAIR TO ELABORATE

"Here is what you need to do to improve your service." It sounds like it would be straightforward, doesn't it? But evidently it really isn't. Lord knows it has been written about a million times in so many management/leadership books. Then why are there still so many funny stories to write about regarding inadequate service? Obviously actions are not speaking out as loud as words.

What does it take to create a workforce that really does enjoy serving customers? Why don't companies take a closer look at their selection practices? Why do companies assume that just anyone in their organization can conduct an interview that garners enough information to make a sound judgment about whether or not someone fits the bill for the open job? The art of interviewing is a special skill set, one for which smart companies mandate management training for.

When are they going to realize that one has to assess during the interview whether or not a candidate really wants to work for a company or might just be coming on board for that weekly paycheck? Is the candidate in alignment with the organization's mission and vision? Pulling out that type of information from a candidate with probing questions is a knack that not everyone has.

Conversely when did the selection process for a new employee turn into being more difficult than getting into the CIA? Does everyone have to have a fourteen-round interview process to get in on the ground floor?

The organizations with higher retention rates and simultaneously, when surveyed, higher employee satisfaction ratings, have four things going for them.

Besides the obvious offerings of:

1. competitive pay scales and
2. comprehensive, creative benefit plans.

They also offer a culture that provides:

3. effective communication and advancement
4. and a great work environment that strives to provide opportunities for employees to give back.

That is, they are customer service-driven organizations that are also community service-oriented from the top down, by the way. This initiative has become increasingly important to the millennial generation of employees.

I wonder how many companies are honestly able to check off all four of the boxes as being priorities in their organizations.

THE B CHAPTER
WHY? BECAUSE IT ENSURES A SMOOTHER TRANSITION

As threaded throughout, what am I going to say is the most important thing a company can do to foster engagement and success in newly hired employees?

Please tell me you got it.

Training, people. There are so many ways to accomplish this that I don't understand why it is so difficult. Does it come down to the almighty dollar? Yes, it costs money, but the benefits reap rewards in the long run. Training can be done in groups, or some might be better suited to being conducted with just one colleague. What about the companies with a mentoring program for new hires? They better make sure to partner the newbie with a mentor who isn't about to quit next Wednesday. Wow, that would make for a great role model. Or worse still, if the mentor spends most of the day complaining about how much the place stinks. Wouldn't that be a nice start for the enthusiastic new hire? Choose the mentors carefully!

How many management books are devoted to the importance of a performance review process? A countless number perhaps?

"Sure, I'll show him around. Right out the
door when I'm done filling him in."

Hmmm, like that happens everywhere. We have all heard of situations, if not having had it happen personally, where the manager cancels on the review meeting day and leaves an email to the effect of "Sorry I had to cancel. Attached is your review

of how I think you are doing. Read it over and send me an email with your feedback." How annoying is that?

Can a company truly be service-oriented if it doesn't have concern for a process to acknowledge and improve its staff's performance? Don't they see the value in sitting down with each and every member of the organization to discuss how he or she is doing? This trend of a lax approach to regular feedback leads to the current tendency of employees feeling undervalued and disposable. Thus, there's no loyalty and high turnover. Hello, people. Thus, there are new hires to train and bring up to speed.

Feedback, an acknowledgement for a job well done as well as areas we need to work on, greatly assists to emphasize the importance of each member's value and alignment to the company goals.

Here is another mystery to me. How can a company expect an employee to serve customers well if they are not kept informed? As noted earlier, communication is one of the top factors that employees say make an organization a great place to work. Why are there so many work environments that function with a veil of secrecy?

"We will communicate on a need-to-know basis." What does that mean anyway? Employees can only be on their best game if they are armed with good information. No one likes being in the dark or uninformed. I believe employees are more effective with the customers they interface with when they are up-to-date on the goings-on at their place of employment.

Some will shudder at my next suggestion. I think a key element to having a service-driven organization is to empower employees to do what it takes to satisfy the customer, even if it means sometimes bending the written rules.

After all, they are the front line with the customer, while their superiors are probably sitting in offices. If the right folks are selected for the job, they will use this authority wisely.

Surely this will save the leadership of the organization from receiving the mountain of disgruntled customer let-ters and cut down on the number of screaming phone calls to their assistants. (Now there is a group that will thank me for bringing this suggestion to the table!) Everyone wins in this case.

Companies that reprimand employees for going out on a limb to satisfy patrons innately send a message of not really trying to covet a service-oriented culture.

THE C CHAPTER
WHY? BECAUSE IT COMES DOWN TO THIS

Even when a company has a thorough selection process and all the training anyone could possibly need, it will still falter without strong leadership.

People are born to be leaders. Oh, of course one can be trained to do certain jobs in upper management roles, but being a true leader is an instinctive skill.

Why is there commonly an undertone that extremely successful field professionals will also be victorious at leading an organization?

I don't believe that this can be presumed to be one in the same. When are companies going to figure out, just because they have a world-renowned surgeon on staff, it doesn't mean he or she will make for an effective hospital administrator? The keen eye for fashion from a retail buyer doesn't necessarily equate to having the skills to manage others, does it? As another example, the extraordinary CFO, who very successfully manages a vast staff of finance employees seamlessly, might not be the best candidate for CEO.

Surely you get where I am going here.

Not everyone has the ability to inspire, cheerlead, and positively push an organization to a higher ground. A leader has the ability to get others motivated to want to do what he or she wants them to do.

I wish more companies would stop talking and start walking.

I would like to see them just try to get through their own telephone systems!

Maybe they would gain some insight if they pretended they were just like you or me, a customer with an issue. That would be an effective technique to understand the steps we are expected to go through.

Somehow and some way, they should get firsthand experience to gain a better understanding of how things currently work in their organization.

I think getting out of the office is a good suggestion, that is, taking a road trip to wherever they have people working to grow their business. How often does the leadership actually spend time out there, listening to their employees' points of view? Aren't these folks their lifeline to the customers they supposedly want to serve?

In my humble opinion, this would be much more valuable to a company's success than sitting at a desk, analyzing reports. Reports tell you where you stand. Being out there tells you why you stand where you stand.

Every company has a mission statement, right? Well, it means absolutely nothing unless it is a true reflection of what is actually taking place on a day-to-day level. I guarantee that most mission statements have a hint, if not a direct reference, about being "service-oriented" or "customer-driven," but it is a smoke screen if you do not have processes and procedures in place to make it happen, training that supports it, and programs that back up these words of wisdom. I think this is commonly where the first breakdown of "just talking and not walking" occurs.

It's a lot to chew on and ponder. Keep out there, striving to make it better. Speak up. I will be.

A tip of the hat to those of you who are successfully making your businesses a truly service-oriented, customer-driven company. Our future depends on you to turn this service complacency around. I and others are counting on you.

While I continue to ponder why companies can't get service right, I am also wondering why you have to explain what erectile dysfunction is to your children because of commercials during an enjoyable Sunday afternoon football game.

CPSIA information can be obtained
at www.ICGtesting.com
Printed in the USA
BVOW03*1629111116
467620BV00001B/1/P

9 781480 838352